Stacey Demarco

2021
LUNAR

& SEASONAL DIARY

Northern Hemisphere

ROCKPOOL
rockpoolpublishing.co

'No thing great is created suddenly, any
more than a bunch of grapes or a fig.
If you tell me you desire a fig, I answer
you that there must be time. Let it first
blossom, then bear fruit, then ripen.'

EPICTETUS, STOIC PHILOSOPHER, 55 AD-135 AD, THE DISCOURSES, 108

A Rockpool book
P.O. Box 252 Summer Hill NSW 2130
Australia
rockpoolpublishing.co
facebook.com/RockpoolPublishing

First published in 2020
Text © Stacey Demarco, 2020
Design © Rockpool publishing, 2020
Internal design by Sara Lindberg, Rockpool Publishing
Edited by Lisa Macken
Cover design by Kinga Britschgi
Author photo by Jason Corroto
Images by Shutterstock

ISBN 978-1-925924-28-2
Northern Hemisphere Edition
Printed and bound in China
10 9 8 7 6 5 4 3 2 1

2021 CALENDAR

JANUARY
M	T	W	T	F	S	S
				1	2	3
4	5	6	7	8	9	10
11	12	13	14	15	16	17
18	19	20	21	22	23	24
25	26	27	28	29	30	31

FEBRUARY
M	T	W	T	F	S	S
1	2	3	4	5	6	7
8	9	10	11	12	13	14
15	16	17	18	19	20	21
22	23	24	25	26	27	28

MARCH
M	T	W	T	F	S	S
1	2	3	4	5	6	7
8	9	10	11	12	13	14
15	16	17	18	19	20	21
22	23	24	25	26	27	28
29	30	31				

APRIL
M	T	W	T	F	S	S
			1	2	3	4
5	6	7	8	9	10	11
12	13	14	15	16	17	18
19	20	21	22	23	24	25
26	27	28	29	30		

MAY
M	T	W	T	F	S	S
					1	2
3	4	5	6	7	8	9
10	11	12	13	14	15	16
17	18	19	20	21	22	23
24	25	26	27	28	29	30
31						

JUNE
M	T	W	T	F	S	S
	1	2	3	4	5	6
7	8	9	10	11	12	13
14	15	16	17	18	19	20
21	22	23	24	25	26	27
28	29	30				

JULY
M	T	W	T	F	S	S
			1	2	3	4
5	6	7	8	9	10	11
12	13	14	15	16	17	18
19	20	21	22	23	24	25
26	27	28	29	30	31	

AUGUST
M	T	W	T	F	S	S
						1
2	3	4	5	6	7	8
9	10	11	12	13	14	15
16	17	18	19	20	21	22
23	24	25	26	27	28	29
30	31					

SEPTEMBER
M	T	W	T	F	S	S
		1	2	3	4	5
6	7	8	9	10	11	12
13	14	15	16	17	18	19
20	21	22	23	24	25	26
27	28	29	30			

OCTOBER
M	T	W	T	F	S	S
				1	2	3
4	5	6	7	8	9	10
11	12	13	14	15	16	17
18	19	20	21	22	23	24
25	26	27	28	29	30	31

NOVEMBER
M	T	W	T	F	S	S
1	2	3	4	5	6	7
8	9	10	11	12	13	14
15	16	17	18	19	20	21
22	23	24	25	26	27	28
29	30					

DECEMBER
M	T	W	T	F	S	S
		1	2	3	4	5
6	7	8	9	10	11	12
13	14	15	16	17	18	19
20	21	22	23	24	25	26
27	28	29	30	31		

INTRODUCTION

Thank you so very much for deciding to flow through a year of lunar and solar energies with me.

This diary is dedicated to those of you who have or are returning to finding a deeper connection with nature and who are seeking to fall in love with the planet over and over.

My gratitude as always to my husband Adam and my agent Richard Martin for their support. A thank you to my publisher and her team at Rockpool Publishing, and to Kinga Britschigi for her beautiful cover.

And to the goddess Artemis, She Who Protects Nature: this work is, as always, part of my devotion to you.

HOW TO USE THIS DIARY

Welcome to a new year and a diary with a difference!

Recently, I found myself in a very remote part of Africa, within a desert environment and a long way from a city. As there was no light pollution, the night sky was very clear. My head lifted literally to the stars and planets; it was so very dark that it was easy to see the celestial spill of the Milky Way spreading across the view. I also noticed the crescent moon, which appeared like a sweet upturned smile, slightly pink and with rosy lips.

I mentioned the shape to a travelling companion who lives in the northern hemisphere (I live in the southern hemisphere) and how the shape of the crescent moon isn't like this where I come from. 'What do you mean the crescent moon isn't like this?' she exclaimed. I explained that the crescent moon didn't look like a smile where I live but was turned on its side, like an opening parenthesis or the letter C, and was lit on the side. 'Well, what do you know! I thought the moon was the same everywhere!'

Most of us don't think that often about the moon so it's understandable that we don't know the moon might appear differently depending on where we are on earth. In Africa we were close to the equator, so the moon was seemingly lit from below. If you're south of the equator and facing north you'll see the moon at its zenith lit from left to right, but we don't have to know the science to love the moon and what it can do for us.

This lunar and seasonal diary gives you all the timings and information I believe are most relevant and effective for modern people to progress themselves and their magic. I never want to be overly complex because we can so easily get wrapped up in analysis paralysis. All the information here can be used in practical ways as the year progresses and changes from month to month and season to season. The clear marking of dark, new and full moon phases throughout the weeks and a daily update on whether the moon is waxing or waning are easy ways to keep on top of the most advantageous energetic timings for everything from spellcasting, growing and harvesting plants and balancing your body to creating personalised ritual. There is a section at the beginning of each month to keep track of your ideas, actions and intentions so you can bring them from thought to reality with more ease and keep real growth happening.

While this diary provides a lot of information for even the most complex workings, it is the simpler things I would advise you to action to give yourself a more robust and deeper connection to the cycles. For example: watch the moon change her shape every night; watch the sun come up or go down often; or feel the expansiveness of the sky by sitting or lying under it and simply allowing the clouds or the swirl of the stars go by. By doing this you'll come to understand you are a part of nature, not apart from nature. Understand that you are, in fact, nature.

You are connected to all beings, all biomes, all cycles, all elements, all atoms, dark matter, electricity, habitats … all of it.

All of it.

It's all magic.

And, so, you *are* the magic too.

With great love,

Stacey Demarco

THE MODERN WITCH

STARTING YOUR
YEAR POSITIVELY

Many people decide they won't even try for new year's intentions any more because they can never keep them. Some people do set unreasonable goals (such as losing huge amounts of weight in one month), but the big reason we don't achieve what we say we want is that, really, we don't want it all that badly.

'I do want it, though!' you might say. 'But I really do want to get healthy, or I really do want that new car/house/job/love!' Here is the big reason why you may not want it all that much: because right now it either doesn't align with your values or you are wanting goals that actually belong to someone else. You simply aren't that devoted or you get distracted.

For some people there is the feeling of: 'What if I get this thing, what then? Will my family still love me? Will this new job actually be better? Will my life change so much that I can't control it any more?'

Take all of that and look at it, feel it. That smells like confusion and fear to me!

To assist you to get clearer about what you *really* want, below is an exercise I get participants in my infamous new year's workshops to do. Fill this out before you do any new year's spells or rituals, and I think you may find you get a big truth bomb hitting you in a very good way. You'll sort out what really matters to you, and you can base your resolutions on that and be devoted to what you want to be rather than what you might be unconsciously doing. You'll be able to track your progress and update it as you grow each month on the month header pages.

I love the gateway of the new year because it is a gateway into a fresh start if you wish it to be so. It's a catalyst for change. Many ancient cultures saw the beginning of a new year as an opportunity to journey through a gateway into something unknown, but to do so meant a leap of faith both literally and figuratively.

The Romans, for example, took this idea literally, creating new year's doorways dedicated to the goddess Jana and the god Janus that people jumped though from one side to another to signify they had indeed left the energy of the previous year behind and fully accepted a new start. The Mayans smashed statues within gateways representing the old year then walked over the rubble to get to the new year gateway.

We can all jump through a new gateway. We can all be brave and courageous and inspired. We can all be leaders and heroes and have happy endings in our own story. So let us begin …

GETTING CLEAR
ABOUT 2021

Here are some great questions to ask yourself to get clear about what you want for 2021.

◆ What are my values? (Values are guiding ideals and principles. Examples of values include honesty, compassion, creativity, calmness, fairness, independence and freedom.)

_____

◆ What are my needs? (Needs are things you must have to be at your best.)

_____

◆ What am I devoted to right now? (You can be devoted to things that are positive or non-positive. You are devoted to what you actually do, for example, if you eat a lot of potato chips then you are devoted to eating potato chips.)

_____

◆ What do I want to be devoted to?

_____

◆ Take those values and needs and think about what would give you the greatest pleasure in 2021.

_____

Let's get even clearer by discerning further based on your values and real pleasures:

◆ What would I definitely wish to leave behind in 2021? (For example, think about old patterns, negative experiences, bad habits, ill health and so on.)

_____

◆ Based on my values and pleasures, what would I love to experience but haven't as yet?

_____

◆ If I could make one positive intention for the community or planet as a whole it would be:

_____

◆ Taking all of this into consideration, the new year's intentions I would love to set are:

_____

◆ My intentions for 2021, stated in January, are:

_____

◆ The steps I will take in January are:

_____

◆ The steps I will take in February are:

_____

◆ The steps I will take in March are:

_____

◆ The steps I will take in April are:

_____

◆ The steps I will take in May are:

_____

◆ The steps I will take in June are:

_____

- The steps I will take in July are:

_____

- The steps I will take in August are:

_____

- The steps I will take in September are:

_____

- The steps I will take in October are:

_____

- The steps I will take in November are:

_____

- The steps I will take in December are:

_____

THE NEW YEAR'S GATEWAY JUMP

Long-time readers of this diary have shared with me how much they love doing the new year's gateway jump. The ancient Romans obviously loved it too, this leaping through the gateway of the new year with the goddess Jana and the god Janus, after whom the month of January was named

This is a fun ritual to do alone or with friends. There are many different versions of the ritual, but all of them involve a physical jump which I think kick starts our mind and spirit.

Ahead of time, find a gateway to jump though. Doorways or gates are perfect, or you can create your own by stretching some pretty fabric between two trees at least 1 metre above head level or by drawing a line in the sand.

Gather together:

+ Some incense to burn.
+ A piece of chalk or a ribbon to mark the gateway jump.
+ A silver candle and a gold candle.
+ A bowl of water with two handfuls of salt added.
+ Your list of intentions for the new year of 2021.

Go to the location of your new year's jump. Burn the incense in a bowl and allow the smoke to purify the area. You might thank the genus loci (the friendly spirits) of the place for their help. When you are done, draw a line with the chalk or place the ribbon across the threshold of the gate or doorway.

LIGHT THE SILVER CANDLE AND SAY: *'Jana of the gateway, goddess of what was and what will be: I am ready to step though 2021 into this brand new creative possibility of 2021. I have thought about my desires and ask you to grant my intentions if they be for the good of all!'*

LIGHT THE GOLD CANDLE AND SAY: *'Janus of the gateway, god of what is behind me and what is in front of me: I am ready to leap excitedly into the future of 2021. Help me achieve my intentions and so much more if it be for the good of all!'*

PLACE YOUR HANDS IN THE BOWL OF SALTED WATER AND SAY: *'In your presence I clear away any burdens or poor actions. I cleanse away my fears and doubts and any obstacles in the way of this new year!'*

Wash your hands, imagining all negative things in your life being cleansed. Read out your intentions for 2021 three times. Be excited about these intentions: don't be shy! Feel that excitement ripple right through your body.

STEP TOWARDS THE GATEWAY OR THRESHOLD AND SAY IN A CLEAR VOICE: *'Jana and Janus: take me through the gateway easily and with your protection. I step forward into the new!'* Step or jump confidently forward through the gateway.

SAY: *'Thank you! Woo hoooo!'* and clap three times loudly.

THANK JANUS AND JANA AND ASK: *'What do I do next?'* Listen for any messages or ideas and act upon them as soon as you can.

Blow out the candles after midnight if possible. Throw the salted water down the drain.

Happy New Year, fellow jumpers!

SPELLCRAFT

How and why do spells work? For a detailed explanation read the relevant chapter in my book *Witch in the Boardroom*, but the short answer depends on whether you wish to go the spiritual or scientific route – or both!

THE SPIRITUAL PATH

Witches and those from many other spiritual paths believe we are connected to all things, including the Divine. The Divine assists us to achieve our intentions through effectively communicating what it is we do or don't want. To perform spellcraft we need to clearly state our intentions and raise considerable energy around the intentions before releasing them in a directed fashion. We then take steps towards what we need and desire and the Divine meets us more than halfway. Magic happens; we get what we want.

THE SCIENTIFIC PATH

Spells speak the language of the subconscious, the part of the mind that directs us towards our goals and dreams. It's where ideas pop up and where creativity is based. You can program your subconscious to focus on what you want through elements such as symbology, movement, visualisation and emotion, and spells are a great way to do this effectively.

Whichever path you choose, know that spells, rituals and invocations do work effectively.

FIVE TOP CASTING TIPS

1. Relax and have fun! One of the best ways to ensure powerful spellcraft is to leave all your administration, worries and preconceived ideas behind and just let go. Spellcraft is meant to be a joyful practice; even when casting to rid ourselves of something we no longer need there is at least a feeling of satisfaction or hope that things will change for the better.

2. Don't worry if things don't go perfectly. So what if the candle blows out or the incense doesn't light or your phone ring: does that mean your spell is ruined? Well, only if you stop! Spells are more about knowing what you want and raising power behind this than whether or not things run perfectly. Be confident, hold your intention clearly and keep going.

3. Plan in advance and be clear about your intention. A quickly planned spell can be a good spell but plan ahead when you can, especially when it comes to timing. This diary gives you great timing information to pinpoint the best days to cast for your particular needs. Ensuring you have any ingredients or supplies ahead of time will reduce your stress levels and leave you free to concentrate on your intentions.

I also think it's important to plan for safety, for example, keeping children and animals away from flames, using good-quality magical supplies (which you may have to order) and having the room well ventilated when using incense. Most important, though, is being crystal clear about what you are casting for, as your intention is of utmost importance. (If you don't know what you want, cast for clarity.) Take time before casting to examine what you do or don't want and put this in clear, concise language. After all, if you don't know what you want the universe can't co-create properly with you.

4. Don't interfere with free will. It is a terrible misconception that witchcraft is commonly used to directly control the mind or actions of other people, when in fact one of the key tenets of most witchcraft traditions is to never interfere with another's free will. Spellcraft works very effectively, so it is not fair to impose our own will or what we believe is the best thing for someone else upon another person or cast on or for other people, as it may have consequences. Even if someone is ill, I always ask permission before commencing any kind of healing invocation. If they are very ill and can't give permission I always add the direction 'If it be for the good of all' as a kind of insurance policy.

Love spells are probably the trickiest when it comes to ensuring free will is intact. No matter what, we never cast for a particular person; instead, we cast for the kind of relationship and partner we desire. This means we attract the best candidate, who may or may not be someone we know!

5. Participate! Participating after the spell is a very important aspect of spellcasting, as it's a chance to get moving in the direction of your intention. After a spell is almost complete I always like to ask the Divine for their suggestions on what to do next. This request is not answered in a big booming voice that clearly tells me what to do; instead, it comes as ideas do, effortlessly and easily, like a 'popping into your head' feeling. By actioning any or all of these messages we are co-creating with the Divine and we start moving. Even a small start has a ripple effect that will lead you more quickly to your intention.

SPELLCASTING MADE EASY

Everyone can spellcast! The spellcasting template below will assist you to write your own effective spell. Each spell has a 'skeleton', or a structure that gives the spell form and function, so fill in the template and you'll have the beginnings of a great spell. And remember: be creative and confident and have fun!

Focus: you have decided to cast a spell for a specific reason and begin to plan the process, taking into consideration time and ethics; it can include a list of things you'll need to cast the spell.

Purpose and intention: clearly and concisely state what the spell is for and what you hope to manifest, such as 'Great goddess, I am here to ask you to help me achieve … quickly and easily' or 'Universe, I wish to attract my ideal partner for a committed relationship leading to marriage.'

Raising power: raise energy to boost your intention; common ways are raising emotion, meditation, drumming, dancing and moving.

Release: release and send out all the power you have raised into the universe; it should be different from how you have raised power such as burning something, clapping, shouting or stopping the movement suddenly.

Participation and grounding: we often feel filled with energy after casting and may wish to ground that energy a little in the physical world; great ways to do this are to have a bath or shower, place our hands on the ground or on a plant or eat something.

THE MOON'S CYCLES AND PHASES

One of the most common questions around spellcasting is: 'What is the best time to cast my spells?'

The simple answer is *any time*, although certain times are more powerful than others; if we align ourselves with them they can assist us in achieving greater success. As we honour the earth and creation we closely observe and are guided by the cycles of nature, including moon cycles, seasonal changes and the position of the sun in the sky.

Traditionally, witches and pagans work closely with moon energy, which encompasses both moon phases and the tides. This diary gives you clear information about moon phases and also offers suggestions about what to cast for. You can check tidal information with your local newspaper, weather channel or specialist website (see the Resources section at the end of this diary).

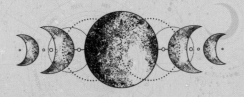

MOON PHASE TIMINGS 2021

DARK MOON	NEW MOON	FULL MOON
12 January	13 January, 12.00 am	28 January, 2.16 pm
10 February	11 February, 2.05 pm	27 February, 3.17 am
12 March	13 March, 5.21 am	28 March, 2.48 pm
10 April	11 April, 10.30 pm	26 April, 11.31 pm
10 May	11 May, 2.59 pm	26 May, 7.13 am
9 June	10 June, 6.52 am	24 June, 2.39 pm
8 July	9 July, 9.16 pm	23 July, 10.36 pm
7 August	8 August, 9.50 am	22 August, 8.01 am
5 September	6 September, 8.51 pm	20 September, 7.54 pm
5 October	6 October, 7.05 am	20 October, 10.56 am
3 November	4 November, 5.14 pm	19 November, 3.57 am
3 December	4 December, 2.43 am	18 December, 11.35 pm

SPECIAL NOTES

- All times are US Eastern Standard Time.
- Time is adjusted for daylight savings time when applicable; adjust for your state/country.
- Dates are based on the Gregorian calendar.

SPECIAL MOON EVENTS

- Super full moon: 26 April.
- Micro new moon: 11 May.
- Super full moon: 26 May.
- Penumbral lunar eclipse visable in New York: 26 May.
- Blue moon: 22 August (third new moon in a season with four new moons).
- Super new moon: 4 November.
- Micro full moon: 19 November.
- Partial lunar eclipse viable in New York: 19 November.
- Super new moon: 4 December.
- Micro full moon: 18 December.

WHAT THE MOON PHASES MEAN

Here is some useful information on what each moon phase means for you in terms of energy, as well as some suggestions on what to cast and when.

FULL MOON

- The moon is full in the sky.
- Full energy! Big energy! Kapow!
- This moon gives you high-impact results and is perfect for attraction spells of any type.
- It's a great time to explore and find your true path and purpose in life.
- Witches formally celebrate their relationship with the Divine once every 28 days during full moon. This is called an esbat, literally a meeting with others in a coven or simply with the Divine.

WANING MOON

- The moon is growing smaller in the sky, which occurs between the full moon and the new moon.
- Energy is reduced.
- It's a good time to perform spells with a purpose and intention of getting rid of something that no longer serves you or to reduce an obstacle.
- It's a great time to give up a bad habit such as an addiction or a limiting or negative belief.

DARK MOON

- No moon is visible in the sky.
- This is traditionally a time of introversion and rest.
- It's a good time for spells that ask for peace and creative flow.
- Experienced witches can use this moon for powerful healing through positive hexing.

NEW MOON

- This occurs the day after the dark moon and is good for fresh starts and renewal.
- This is traditionally the time to make seven wishes.
- It is a great time for spells of health and for the beginning of projects or businesses.
- It's a powerful time to cast spells for better mental health.

Waxing moon

- The moon is growing larger in the sky, which happens between the new moon and the full moon.
- Energy is growing and expanding.
- It's a good time to perform spells with a purpose and intention of growth and moving towards something you desire.
- It's a powerful time to ask for more money, more positive relationships and better health.
- Wonderful for prosperity spells.
- Perfect for asking for bodily vitality, a pay rise, a new job or more recognition.

TIDES

As most people know, tides are linked to the moon. The rise and fall of the tides can be used as additional elements in your spells; aligning them with your spells can make the spells even more powerful. Being by the sea or water and seeing the tides ebb and flow will always add an extra dimension to your spell or ritual.

High tide

- This tide brings things towards you, and is known for attraction.
- It's wonderful for prosperity spells.
- It's perfect for asking for better health, a pay rise, a new job or more recognition.

Low tide

- This tide removes things, takes things away.
- It's perfect for removing obstacles, negative feelings, pain, bad memories and office politics.

King tide

- These are very high and low tides that happen on a regular basis.
- Energies are even more emphasised, so make sure what you are asking for is what you truly desire.
- It may be worth 'saving up' a desire for a king tide if it is a request that can wait.

ASTROLOGICAL CORRESPONDENCES FOR KEY MOON PHASES 2021

MONTH	ASTROLOGICAL SIGN	NEW MOON	FULL MOON
January	Capricorn	13 January, 12.00 am	
	Leo		28 January, 2.16 pm
February	Aquarius	11 February, 2.05 pm	
	Virgo		27 February, 3.17 am
March	Pisces	13 March, 5.21 am	
	Libra		28 March, 2.48 pm
April	Aries	11 April, 10.30 pm	
	Scorpio		26 April, 11.31 pm
May	Taurus	11 May, 2.59 pm	
	Sagittarius		26 May, 7.13 am
June	Gemini	10 June, 6.52 am	
	Capricorn		24 June, 2.39 pm
July	Cancer	9 July, 9.16 pm	
	Aquarius		23 July, 10.36 pm
August	Leo	8 August, 9.50 am	
	Aquarius		22 August, 8.01 am
September	Virgo	6 September, 8.51 pm	
	Pisces		20 September, 7.54 pm
October	Libra	6 October, 7.05 am	
	Aries		20 October, 10.56 am
November	Scorpio	4 November, 5.14 pm	
	Taurus		19 November, 3.57 am
December	Sagittarius	4 December, 2.43 am	
	Gemini		18 December, 11.35 pm

BENEFICIAL TIMINGS

DAWN

- New beginnings.
- New projects.
- Creativity spells.
- Initiations.

SUNSET

- Completions.
- Asking for help for a project or issue that may be long or difficult.
- Spells for faith and preparation.

MIDDAY

- Asking for increased personal power.
- Asking for confidence and strength.
- Asking for the courage to allow your light to shine.
- Worshipping during fire festivals such as Litha.

MIDNIGHT

- The witching hour.
- Asking for self-knowledge.
- Asking for deep and lasting change.
- Asking for help from your ancestors.
- Turning dreams into reality.

EQUINOX AND SOLSTICE UNIVERSAL TIMINGS (UTC)

- Spring equinox (Ostara), 22 September, 7.21 pm
- Summer solstice (Litha), 21 December, 3.59 pm
- Fall equinox (Mabon), 20 March, 9.37 am
- Winter solstice (Yule), 21 June, 3.32 am

EQUINOX AND SOLSTICE EST TIMINGS (DAYLIGHT SAVINGS ADJUSTED)

- Spring equinox (Ostara), 20 March, 5.37 am EDT
- Summer solstice (Litha), 20 June, 11.32 pm EDT
- Fall equinox (Mabon), 22 September, 3.21 pm EDT
- Winter solstice (Yule), 21 December, 10.59 am EST

THE MOON'S TRANSITS WITHIN ASTROLOGICAL SIGNS

Separate to the meanings of the phases of the moon and the timings of the Wheel of the Year, there is an added layer of meaning where the moon is transiting within the signs of the zodiac. The moon makes a full transit of the earth and the signs every two and a half days.

Listed below are the astrological phases of the moon and some corresponding themes around which magical workings can be performed very effectively.

CAPRICORN

When the moon is in Capricorn it is an excellent time for magic concerning planning, clarity, strategy, career and purpose, status and obstacle busting.

AQUARIUS

When the moon is in Aquarius it is an excellent time for magical workings concerning popularity, strengthening friendships, change, creativity, science and deepening spirituality and for the greater good.

PISCES

When the moon is in Pisces it is a beneficial time for magical workings concerning dreams, completion, increasing psychic ability and intuition and flow. It is also a good time to do healing work around women's cycles.

ARIES

When the moon is in Aries it is a beneficial time for magical workings concerning stamina, leadership, dealing with authority figures, strength and study.

TAURUS

When the moon is in Taurus it is an excellent time for magical workings concerning family and children, love, home matters, the purchase of real estate and creating sacred space in the home.

GEMINI

When the moon is in Gemini it is a great time for magical workings concerning expansion, communication of all kinds, travel, writing and invocations.

CANCER

When the moon is in Cancer it is a great time for magical workings concerning all kinds of emotional healing and cutting cords of old relationships. It is also an optimum time for healing the body and promoting health, particularly through diet.

LEO

When the moon is in Leo it is an excellent time for magical workings concerning self-esteem, personal power, status, authority of all kinds and improving the relationship with your boss.

VIRGO

When the moon is in Virgo it is a beneficial time for magical workings concerning getting or keeping a job, exams, purification, clearing and detoxing of all kinds.

LIBRA

When the moon is in Libra it is an excellent time for magical workings concerning balance, justice, all legal matters, better health and weight balance.

SCORPIO

When the moon is in Scorpio it is a great time for magical workings concerning all sexual matters, healing trauma, reducing gossip and increasing fun.

SAGITTARIUS

When the moon is in Sagittarius it is an excellent time for magical workings concerning truth, exposing dishonesty and clarity and asking for increased travel or protection during travel.

ELEMENTS AND DIRECTIONS

You might wish to utilise the elements and directions in your spells and workings to give yet another layer of powerful symbology and energy. Experienced witches use a compass if they are not sure of the directions when setting up a circle (normally, there is one within your mobile phone).

Here are some suggestions for ways of honouring each direction along with corresponding elements, but ultimately the combinations are up to you and will depend on the surrounding geography. There used to be very strict correspondences highly influenced by the northern hemisphere; however, pagans and witches all over the world now combine the elements and directions in the way that the surrounding geography most calls for.

North/earth

- Salt, earth, oils such as oak moss, patchouli.
- Standing on earth, sprinkling of earth and salt, anointing stones.
- Represents resilience, order, law, politics, education, security, money.
- Green/brown.
- Night.

South/fire

- Candles, open flame of any kind, oils such as pepper, ginger, frankincense.
- Lighting flame, passing flame around the circle, anointing with oil.
- Represents passion, purpose, strength, achievement, destruction of what is not needed.
- Masculine – sun.
- Red.
- Noon.

East/air

- Incense, fragrance, smoke, kites, balloons, oils such as bergamot, lime, eucalyptus.
- Smudging, blowing smoke, bubbles, bells, singing bowls.
- Represents communication, creativity, logic, travel, new beginnings, ideas, flow.
- Yellow.
- Dawn.

West/water

- Salt water, moon water, shells, rain, oils such as rose, ylang ylang.
- Anointing with water, passing the cup.
- Represents relationships, love, psychic connection, birth/death/rebirth.
- Feminine – moon.
- Blue.

THE WHEEL OF THE YEAR

As the path of the witch is an earth-based faith, the witches' *sabbats* or holidays are intrinsically connected to the cycles of nature. Primarily, the themes of birth, death and rebirth are played out across a year that is divided into light and dark, male and female, sun and moon, growth and rest and heat and cold.

Most celebrations were traditionally linked to the cycles of the northern hemisphere, so for southern hemisphere witches it became confusing. Do we follow the traditional Wheel of the Year timings even though they are opposite to our seasons, or do we adapt and reverse the wheel so it is in rhythm with our own environment?

Like most witches in the southern hemisphere, I follow the wheel so that it more closely fits our own unique natural seasonal cycles. For this diary, I have aligned the celebrations along these dates.

Importantly, these sacred times connect you with the light, land and with the seasons. The land is our mother; she feeds us, shelters us and gives us comfort and joy. The festivals give us a chance to give something back to her and honour all that she does. As modern people we often forget this and feel disconnected without quite knowing why.

The continuous cycle of nature lends itself to the image of a wheel. The ancient Celts and their predecessors saw time as a wheel or as a spiral divided by eight festivals, listed below. Modern witches can use the themes of each celebration to do magical workings of their own in complete synergy with the natural cycles. The dates featured on solstices/equinoxes are to be used as a guide only, so please refer to the diary itself for accuracy.

Note: Where these festivals fall within the calendar spreads within this diary I have given further information on the festival and some suggestions about how to celebrate the Sabbath with meaning.

SAMHAIN (HALLOWEEN)

- Southern hemisphere 30 April; northern hemisphere 31 October.
- Celebration of death as a continuation of life.
- Borders between the dead and living are not fixed and impassable.
- The veil between the worlds are at their thinnest so one can ask the ancestors and spirits for guidance and communication on the future.
- Celebrating where you came from.
- Traditional time for scrying.
- Witches' new year!

YULE (WINTER SOLSTICE)

- Southern hemisphere 21-23 June; northern hemisphere 21-23 December.
- Longest night of the year.
- Mid-winter festival linked to the Christian Christmas.
- Archetypally linked with the birth of a child of promise and light: Dionysus, Arthur, Jesus, Baldur.
- Celebrates the return of the sun and thus hope.
- Abundance spells and charms.
- Giving thanks and gifts of goodwill.

IMBOLC (CANDLEMAS)

- Southern hemisphere 1 August; northern hemisphere 1 February.
- Celebration of light returning.
- Goddess as Brigid (St Brigid).
- Fire festival.
- Clarity and healing.
- Light to shine, self-knowledge/creation.

OSTARA (SPRING EQUINOX)

- Southern hemisphere 21-23 September; northern hemisphere 21-23 March.
- Night and day are equal, but moving towards summer.
- Balance and growth.
- Leave what you don't want and create the new.
- Fertility and love.
- New projects.

BELTANE (MAY DAY)

- Southern hemisphere 31 October; northern hemisphere 30 April/1 May.
- Marriage of the goddess and the god.
- Maypoles, phallic and yonic symbolism.
- Love magic (weddings/hand fastings).
- Animus and anima/masculine and feminine balances.

LITHA (SUMMER SOLSTICE)

- Southern hemisphere 21-23 December; northern hemisphere 21-23 June.
- Longest day, shortest night.
- Sun is at its fullest power yet the year begins to wane from here.
- What brings light and joy into your life and develops this.
- Self-development.
- Celebration of the masculine divine.

LAMMAS (LUGHNASADH)

- Southern hemisphere 1 February; northern hemisphere 1 August.
- First harvest, first loaf baked.
- The god begins his journey into the underworld.
- Sorrow and celebration.
- Fruition, taking stock and harvesting what you have achieved.

MABON (AUTUMN EQUINOX)

- Southern hemisphere 21-22 March; northern hemisphere 21-22 September.
- Harvesting the main crop.
- Take stock of what has/has not served you well.
- What needs repairing before the dark comes.
- Preparation for harder times.
- Welcoming change energy.

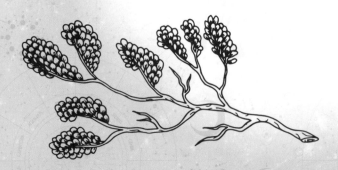

YOUR BODY AND THE MOON

We are moon-influenced animals even if most of us don't go howling under it! Long-held knowledge indicates a number of ways the moon can impact our physical bodies.

DETOXING

Many of us at some stage feel the need to re-energise the body through a detox of some sort. Usually it's after a period of overindulgence: perhaps too much rich food, alcohol or sugar. Detoxes became quite fashionable and all kinds of weird and wacky systems and products are now being promoted. I am not a big fan of detoxing in its newest, most faddish form, but if a detox to you means a period of consuming more deeply nourishing food in smaller quantities, less stimulants and alcohol and more sleep, I am all for it!

Should you decide a detox is something you do wish to undertake, the moon can help you make this time more successful.

ONE-DAY DETOXES

Early on the day before a new moon (dark moon), set an intention that over the next 24 hours you will release what your body does not need. Upon waking on the new moon day, set an intention to release all that you don't need and start your detox.

LONGER DETOXES

Begin your program on a full moon, setting an intention that as the moon wanes so will the toxins be released from your body. Continue your program during the waning period but no longer.

Note: unless you are sure you are fit enough to embark on a detox program, do not attempt to do it yourself. Seek professional advice.

WEIGHT BALANCE

Setting your intention and beginning your healthy weight program on a full moon is a great idea as it gets your mind used to the idea that this is something you want. You might even cast a spell for health and vitality that night to boost it along. (There is a good spell free on my website www.themodernwitch.com.)

Begin your program straight after a full moon and notice that the moon is waning, taking with it extra weight and fluid. You will lose more weight more rapidly during a waning moon.

When the moon becomes a new moon you should do another ritual to boost your intention. Lighting a candle and simply asking the universe to continue to assist you to reach your goal and achieve greater health is enough.

You must be careful not to eat foods during a waxing moon cycle that are not aligned with your intention, as these cycles will hold them to the body far more than during waning cycles. However, you will generally have more energy during waxing moons so this is the time to boost your activity levels and burn off what you consume more easily.

When the moon becomes full again, be grateful for what you have achieved or achieved so far and set your intention moving forward.

HAIR

I know many lunartics love cutting and growing your hair by the moon cycles, and I also know that full and new moon days are some of the most popular days in hairdressers all over the world! It is thought that different phases influence hair growth just as they influence tides, so it's no surprise that full and waxing moons are best friends to those of us who want longer locks.

GROWING YOUR HAIR

Traditionally, should you wish to grow your hair, cut it only when it is in its most active phase during a full or waxing moon.

If you wish to keep your hair the same length (very handy for those who have a fringe or short hair), cut it on a waning moon.

STRENGTHENING YOUR HAIR

Try new moon days and waxing moons to apply treatments to your hair.

For the mother of all good hair days go for a full moon in Cancer for all your conditioning and cutting treatments.

HAIR REMOVAL

Whether you wax, laser or shave, the best time to remove hair is during a waning moon cycle. It will stay away for longer.

BALANCING BODY CYCLES

There is some excellent research available on the correlation of lunar light, moon phases and bodily biorhythms such as those related to our hormonal and fertility cycles. There seem to be two camps on this: one that sees no correlation with the moon cycles of 28-29 days with the typical female cycle of the same length or with a spike in fertility around the full moon, and another that recognises this long-held wisdom as fact.

If you have a menstrual cycle that is radically less or more than 29 days you may consider it beneficial to balance your cycle. To do this, watch the moon for five minutes each night. You need light to activate a whole cascade of bodily functions, and the fertility cycle is but one of them. If you wish, you could visualise your most fertile time at a full moon (full power!) and your wise blood flowing around a dark/new moon (letting go, starting afresh).

THE LUNAR RETURN

Across a number of ancient cultures such as the Egyptian and Sumerian it was believed the moon phase upon birth triggered the beginning of life and remained as a person's peak time energetically throughout life. This was especially evident for women, as it determined their most fertile time. Sumerian medicine records indicate a belief that a woman was most fertile when the moon was at the same phase as her birth. Ancient Celts and Egyptians recorded the moon phase at birth and told both sexes when they came of age. This is called a lunar return.

A lunar return is not what astrological moon sign you were born in; it's more astronomy than astrology! Rather, it's what actual phase was in the sky upon your birth, for example, full moon, quarter moon, two days before a new moon and so on.

Until fairly recently the accepted science was that women had a covert cycle of ovulation. This referred to a hidden set time, usually at the centre of the cycle, but with no overt obvious clues such as your cat or dog might display when on heat. Science indicated there was only one small fertile time in a human woman's cycle and that it had to be around that centre point. However, there have been some recent studies that indicate the contrary: that lots of exposure to sex/men can cause spontaneous ovulation at any time in the month. Further studies are now being undertaken to see if there is any pattern to this within diet and light exposure. Perhaps in this case old wisdom is true wisdom!

If you are male this also includes you. Scientists believe men have a fertility biorhythm and it could well be related to light and frequency of sex.

The simple idea of knowing which phase of the moon you were born during as well as keeping an eye on the moon regularly seems to induce more hormonal balance in both sexes, and is very useful if you are wishing to conceive (or not). If you are interested in more thorough information about the moon and fertility and how to best take advantage of this you might like to read my book *Witch in the Bedroom*.

Wouldn't you like to know when you are physically and mentally at your best, or when you are at the top of your game for sport, exams or decision-making? Knowing when you will be feeling most vital and energetic really does have profound impacts on everyday life.

LUNAR/SOLAR ENERGY
AND CRYSTALS

Utilising crystals to focus and capture energy is something that both pagan and non-pagan practitioners do. One of the most popular ways of cleansing and charging your crystals is to place them under the moonlight. However, there are some subtle ways of enhancing crystal energy by matching the specific lunar energy at certain times in the cycle or by using solar energy.

LUNAR ENERGY

Cleansing: leave your crystals out under the power of a full moon or waxing moon. If you are using the powers of a waxing moon, leave the crystals out on multiple nights right up to the full moon.

Dedicating for matters of prosperity: I have had success with leaving crystals out in the moonlight in a bowl of shallow water. The water promotes the flow of money towards you.

Dedicating for matters of growth: place your crystals on living soil or a plant. Grass is perfect, as is a healthy pot plant. Leave the crystals out under moonlight and then leave them out for a full day of sunshine as well.

Dedicating to absorb negative energies: many crystals are useful to us in the way they help us dispel or absorb negative energies; jet, obsidian, black tourmaline and pink kunzite are good examples of this. Give these crystals an extra boost by dedicating them or charging them on a dark or waning moon cycle.

Dedicating for meditation or channelling: I very much like to dedicate stones such as lapis, amethyst, clear quartz or turquoise during dark moons when the energies are aligned for more introverted, inward-facing activities. I like to take these crystals into the darker parts of my garden or even into areas shaded slightly by rocks but still able to be graced by the sky. I try and retrieve them just before dawn to keep the integrity of the darkness intact.

SOLAR ENERGY

While I love to leave my crystals out basking in the silvery moonlight, there are some crystals that thrive under the fiery sun. I find that naturally gold or warm-coloured stones such as amber and citrine often need a good dose of solar energy to keep them happy, so don't be afraid to do so. When dedicating your crystals you will still need to cleanse them first in whichever manner works best for you, but here are some charging and dedication suggestions using solar energy that work for me.

Dedicating for health: on three consecutive days, leave your crystals that will be dedicated to health and healing out from dawn until dusk. Mid-summer is an ideal time to do this, as is the time around a new moon.

Dedicating for inspiration: get a boost from the biggest fire of all to fan your personal fires of inspiration: the sun. Place your stones on a natural surface such as grass or a plant and leave them out from dawn until dusk for seven days. Springtime is a great time to do this each year.

Gifts: when I am giving a crystal to a man I always leave it out under the sun for a day or so. The sun gives the stone a charging of masculine energy that I believe enables it to bind more quickly to its new owner. For women, leave your crystal under the moon instead.

PLANTS AND THE MOON

People all over the planet have been farming and gardening by the moon's cycles for millennia. The earth operates under a gravity field that is influenced by the moon (and also by other planets), which affects the growth of plants. Just as the moon influences the oceans and other bodies of water, it is believed the moon changes the level of water in the soil, affecting seedling and plant growth.

There are amazing farmer's almanacs you can buy for your region each year that give very detailed planting suggestions and harvesting recommendations, all guided by the moon and astrological information. (Check the Resources section at the end of the book for details.)

This isn't a gardening diary but I have added some suggestions, and it certainly is worth mentioning the basic rules of thumb when it comes to gardening by the moon. As more and more of us choose to grow our own organic herbs, vegies and other plants, knowing how the moon may influence your patch could make the difference between a fair, good or bumper crop.

FULL MOON

As the water rises and swells within the soil it is a perfect time to plant seeds. It is also a good time to harvest some plants at the peak of their goodness.

WANING MOON

As the water level sinks it's time for planting your below-ground plants such as potatoes, carrots, onions, parsnips and beetroot.

NEW MOON

Growth slows with the new moon, so this is the time to prune, trim, weed and fertilise. Apply any necessary natural pest control.

WAXING MOON

This is growth time again, as water begins to rise. It is a good time for planting your above-ground crops such as pumpkin, tomatoes, cauliflower, kale, lettuce and spinach.

FERTILE ZODIAC SIGNS

Water and earth signs are considered to be the growth times for plants. When the moon enters these signs it's a fine time to plant or prune back for growth.

BARREN ZODIAC SIGNS

All your maintenance chores should be done when the moon is in fire and air signs.

JANUARY

- ◆ What would I like to create, experience and manifest this month?

_____

_____

_____

_____

- ◆ What are the important dates for me this month?

_____

_____

- ◆ What would give me joy this month?

_____

_____

- ◆ What am I devoted to?

_____

_____

- ◆ Ideas, musings, actions:

_____

_____

_____

PAN

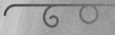

At the beginning of each year I love to set intentions for growth, expansiveness and happiness. This means I start the year off with momentum of a more joyful kind, without pressure or stress. This year I thought we could start January off with a god who I think is quite underestimated in these areas.

Pan is the ancient Greek god of wild places, shepherds, mountains and fertility. Shaggy and unkempt in appearance and with long hair, a goat's lower half and a button nose, what Pan lacked in classic looks he made up for in energy, charm and musical ability. Depictions of Pan often showed him with an erect phallus, just in case people didn't recognise his sexual energy and wildness.

Pan was the patron protector of shepherds, as these folk would have been one of the only people regularly outside in the rougher and more rustic mountain places. Pan was a god who could be found in thick forest, in snowy mountains, in rocky crags, by the groves of streams and in lonely outdoor places where few travelled. He would be busy all morning hunting, watching over his people and making love, then would require a decent afternoon nap. If disturbed, it would make him very angry and he would unleash an almighty screeching noise that would frighten people and send them into a 'pan-ic'.

Invite Pan into your life when you need a boost to your fertility and joyfulness. Re-wilding yourself is a positive thing, and Pan urges you to play and find your bliss sensually, sexually and creatively. He is a big energy to work with and one that you can especially find in vigorous dancing, music and movement.

I highly recommend that if you find yourself in Greece that you make the effort not only to visit the famous oracle site of Delphi, which is within old Arcadia, but perhaps the less known but hugely powerful Corycian Cave, a place of Pan on the other side of the sacred mountain of Mt Parnassas. The locals still play music seasonally in the cave and have celebration picnics there, particularly around the time of a full moon.

INVOCATION TO PAN

THIS INVOCATION IS MUCH MORE EFFECTIVE IF YOU GO OUTSIDE INTO NATURE TO CAST IT. IF YOU PLAY AN INSTRUMENT, FEEL FREE TO DO SO.

Obtain a green crystal or sand stone. Cast yourself a circle and hold the stone.

SAY: *'Great Pan, goat-footed, horned god, son of Hermes, ally of Zeus, ruler of the wild woods, friend of shepherds, ruler of Arcadia, player in high places: hear me!'*

SPIN IN A CIRCLE AND SAY: *'Show me my healthy wildness. Show me the joy of life. Shower me with growth and fertility.'*

SPIN AND SAY: *'Fill me with music, fill me with song. Inspire me with bliss and joy. Re-wild my quiet nature. Remind me of the pleasure I deserve.'*

Spin! Spin Spin!

If you have a request of Pan for the year, request it now. Listen for any messages.

Leave the stone within the circle for next time.

28 Monday ◖

Waxing

29 Tuesday, ◯ full moon in Cancer 10.28 pm EST

This is the last full moon of the yearm so make it count!

30 Wednesday

Waning

31 Thursday

Waning

New Year's Eve spell: set your intentions for 2021 if you haven't already done so. Do the spell with Jana and Janus of the gateway or mark the end of this year with a small ritual of gratitude before you go out to celebrate. Merely lighting a candle with intention and giving a special honouring of all the energies or deities that assisted you this year is a great start.

1 Friday

Waning

Welcome to a new year!

Catch the wave of global 'fresh start, new beginnings' energy. Release your intentions today!

2 Saturday

Waning

3 Sunday

Waning

DECEMBER								JANUARY						
M	T	W	T	F	S	S		M	T	W	T	F	S	S
	1	2	3	4	5	6						1	2	3
7	8	9	10	11	12	13		4	5	6	7	8	9	10
14	15	16	17	18	19	20		11	12	13	14	15	16	17
21	22	23	24	25	26	27		18	19	20	21	22	23	24
28	**29**	**30**	**31**					25	26	27	28	29	30	31

4 Monday ◑

Waning

5 Tuesday ◑

Waning

6 Wednesday ◑

Waning

7 Thursday ◑

Waning

8 Friday

Waning

Friday was named after the Norse goddess of love and magic, Freya.

9 Saturday

Waning

10 Sunday

Waning

You are your own dawn.

- THE GODDESS

JANUARY

M	T	W	T	F	S	S
				1	2	3
4	5	6	7	8	9	10
11	12	13	14	15	16	17
18	19	20	21	22	23	24
25	26	27	28	29	30	31

11 Monday

Waning

12 Tuesday

Dark moon

It is the beginning of an exciting new year, so here is your chance to release what you do not want to bring through!

13 Wednesday, ☽ new moon in Capricorn, 12.00 am EST

A great time to set intentions to start long-term new projects and for resilience and stability.

14 Thursday ◐

Waxing

15 Friday ◑

Waxing

16 Saturday ◑

Waxing

17 Sunday ◑

Waxing

JANUARY						
M	T	W	T	F	S	S
				1	2	3
4	5	6	7	8	9	10
11	12	13	14	15	16	17
18	19	20	21	22	23	24
25	26	27	28	29	30	31

18 Monday

Waxing

19 Tuesday

Waxing

20 Wednesday

Waxing

21 Thursday

Waxing

If you wish to grow your hair, this is a great time to trim it to promote growth.

22 Friday ◐

Waxing

23 Saturday ◐

Waxing

24 Sunday ◐

Waxing

25 Monday ◐

Waxing

26 Tuesday ◐

Waxing

27 Wednesday ◐

Waxing

28 Thursday, ○ full moon in Leo, 2.16 pm EST

Take advantage of this big energy and set intentions to boost your personal power and positive leadership.
How are those new year's intentions going?

29 Friday

Waning

30 Saturday

Waning

31 Sunday

Waning

It is the festival of Imbolc tomorrow. Leave out a bowl of water for Brigid to bless for your health and beauty.

Joyfully step forward with confidence for you are made of the stuff of stars.

- THE GODDESS

JANUARY

M	T	W	T	F	S	S
				1	2	3
4	5	6	7	8	9	10
11	12	13	14	15	16	17
18	19	20	21	22	23	24
25	26	27	28	29	30	31

FEBRUARY

- ◆ What would I like to create, experience and manifest this month?

_____

_____

_____

_____

- ◆ What are the important dates for me this month?

_____

_____

- ◆ What would give me joy this month?

_____

_____

- ◆ What am I devoted to?

_____

_____

- ◆ Ideas, musings, actions:

_____

_____

_____

LEUTOGI

GODDESS OF THE MONTH: FEBRUARY

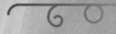

Wouldn't it be a powerful act if we could all be kinder to each other?
Royalty from the Samoan Islands, Princess Leutogi was sent to Tonga to become the second wife of the-then king of Tonga. It was not a love match, as she was sent as part of a peace treaty through marriage between the kingdoms. Although sealing alliances through marriage was a common practice, often the wives were treated badly and looked down upon by the community. Unfortunately, Leutogi was indeed treated badly.

One day as she walked through the gardens Leutogi discovered a baby bat that was sick and wounded. She was a kind and gentle woman, and in her mercy looked after the little bat until it was well again then released it back to its colony.

This act didn't remain a secret, as the royal court watched everything Leutogi did. The court laughed at her kindness and thought her weak and stupid, which made her an easy target when the king's fortunes declined. The royal court suggested that it was Leutogi who caused the king's problems, and they decided to kill her by burning her on a pyre.

The flames were lit and rose to engulf Leutogi when suddenly the sky darkened. The baby bat and his family had not forgotten the kindness of the princess and had come to help her. Thousands upon thousands of bats flew above the fire, urinating down on the flames to extinguish them. Leutogi was saved, but her trials were not yet over. Frustrated, the Tongan king exiled her to a very small island with nothing to eat. The island was completely barren, so the king and his court were sure that Leutogi would soon starve. Again, the fruit bats assisted her by bringing food, including fruits and seeds, and they kept her happy with their smiling company.

Soon the island became one of fertility and plenty as many of the bats made it their new home. The kind princess was very happy, and she transformed into a goddess of plenty and fertility and the patroness protector of all bats.

Meditation for kindness

We could all do with a bit more kindness in our lives. The ideal place to invoke this beautiful kind energy is outside under a tree on a beach. You'll need a flower for your hair and a piece of jewellery.

Allow yourself to relax, whether you are sitting or lying down. Breathe deeply. Imagine you are in a beautiful lush rainforest; open up in all your senses to the forest. There you can see the goddess Leutogi and her fruit bat friends. They are flying around happily and perching in trees with their babies. The forest is full of flowers and food, and is a calm and peaceful place.

SAY: *'Leutogi, you who chose kindness over hatred, you who showed mercy over turning away, show me how to embody kindness in thoughts, in deeds and in actions.'*

Now Leutogi is coming towards you and smiling gently at you. You hand her your piece of jewellery. She holds it to her heart, kisses it and hands it back to you, then she holds your face or hands in both of hers. You feel the loving kindness she embodies and this is shared with you. Allow it to fill you. Think of where you would like more kindness in your life and know that the kindness is now there.

Think about extending that kindness outwards to others, to the world, to all beings. Know that things have changed for the better. You can come back to this place and Leutogi whenever you wish.

Open your eyes and place the flower in your hair and wear the jewellery that is now a talisman of kindness.

WHEEL OF THE YEAR

Imbolc

Wake up; it is here!

I always feel the time coming up to Imbolc before I see it. You can feel the earth waking up from her winter slumber: there is no more sleepy, quiet energy and something is stirring – it's the earth!

We are approaching the festival of Imbolc on 1st August. Imbolc is one of the eight festivals of the witches' year and is a celebration of the returning of the light after the depths of winter. It's the perfect time to ask for clarity of purpose and to increase self-knowledge, thus allowing your true light to shine.

Originally it was a celebration particularly honouring the Celtic goddess Brigid in her fiery spring aspect. This beginning of the change of season was considered to be the time that Brigid's fire sparks again and awakens the earth. It is also the time that our own personal fires ignite our passions once again and we begin to take more action, burn away our doubts and delve deeper into our own creativity. There is a feeling of optimism and quiet joy about Imbolc time: baby animals are born and plants are beginning to push through the barren ground of winter.

An Imbolc altar is a beautiful altar! I decorate mine in silver, gold and red and always include lots of fresh seasonal flowers, including buds. Beforehand I thoroughly wash the altar and the surrounds and burn fragrant herbs such as mint, rosemary and sage. Using rose water is a particular lovely way to clean.

Something very traditional to try is creating Brigid's cross, a way of honouring the goddess and calling in good luck for your home. It's a simple but very lovely activity and all you need is some straw or small flexible twigs from your garden. Get on the internet to quickly learn how to create the cross; it's a great thing to do with kids as well. I hang the crosses as decorations on the trees in my garden ready for Imbolc morning.

This is my favorite tradition for Imbolc: leaving water out for Brigid's blessing. Leave out a bowl containing a small amount of fresh water on the night before Imbolc. Also leave out freshly baked cakes or cream, honey or milk as a gift for her.

Brigid will come around and bless the water herself, and any dew that forms that morning will also be powerfully blessed by spring energies. These healing waters blessed by the goddess herself are powerful if you wash your face with them; in the spirit of renewal and rebirth, it is said that if you wash your face in the water you will not age for another year. Beats an expensive face cream, right?

1 Monday, ◐ Imbolc

Waning

Imbolc: the light is retWaning! May the blessings of Brigid be upon you. If you have collected it, use the goddess Bridgid's Imbolc healing waters for your health and potions.

2 Tuesday ◐

Waning

3 Wednesday ◐

Waning

4 Thursday ◐

Waning

5 Friday

Waning

6 Saturday

Waning

7 Sunday

Waning

Joyous flowing focus is available to you at any time you choose.

- THE GODDESS

FEBRUARY

M	T	W	T	F	S	S
1	**2**	**3**	**4**	**5**	**6**	**7**
8	9	10	11	12	13	14
15	16	17	18	19	20	21
22	23	24	25	26	27	28

8 Monday ◗

Waning

9 Tuesday ◗

Waning

10 Wednesday ●

Dark moon

Breathe and go within. Relax in the void of the dark moon.

11 Thursday, ☽ new moon in Aquarius, 2.05 pm EST

Ask for inventiveness and a bigger, more expansive view on all you are doing.

12 Friday

Waxing

13 Saturday

Waxing

14 Sunday

Waxing

Happy Lupercalia! (Valentine's Day)

Forget Valentine's Day and listen to the tale of Lupercalia. The ancient Roman festival of Lupercalia celebrated virility, wildness, fertility and lust. Today, ride the energetic wave of love of what is now called Valentine's Day and cast a love spell to improve your current relationship or to attract a new one that suits you perfectly.

FEBRUARY

M	T	W	T	F	S	S
1	2	3	4	5	6	7
8	**9**	**10**	**11**	**12**	**13**	**14**
15	16	17	18	19	20	21
22	23	24	25	26	27	28

15 Monday

Waxing

16 Tuesday

Waxing

17 Wednesday

Waxing

18 Thursday

Waxing

19 Friday

Waxing

20 Saturday

Waxing

21 Sunday

Waxing

You are the spark that lived inside of me that now lives within you.
Pass it on.

– THE GODDESS

FEBRUARY

M	T	W	T	F	S	S
1	2	3	4	5	6	7
8	9	10	11	12	13	14
15	**16**	**17**	**18**	**19**	**20**	**21**
22	23	24	25	26	27	28

22 Monday

Waxing

23 Tuesday

Waxing

24 Wednesday

Waxing

25 Thursday

Waxing

26 Friday

Waxing

27 Saturday, ◯ full moon in Virgo, 3.17 am EST

Make this a simple devotional time: you know what you want, so set clear intentions and ask and act.

28 Sunday ◑

Waning

FEBRUARY

M	T	W	T	F	S	S
1	2	3	4	5	6	7
8	9	10	11	12	13	14
15	16	17	18	19	20	21
22	**23**	**24**	**25**	**26**	**27**	**28**

MARCH

◆ What would I like to create, experience and manifest this month?

_____

_____

_____

_____

◆ What are the important dates for me this month?

_____

_____

◆ What would give me joy this month?

_____

_____

◆ What am I devoted to?

_____

_____

◆ Ideas, musings, actions:

_____

_____

_____

ANANSI

GOD OF THE MONTH: MARCH

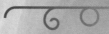

Before the time of writing or the kinds of electronic communication tools we have come to accept as no great miracle, people learnt and spread news orally. It usually involved the community sitting around a fire and the orator, bard or storytellers singing and expressively sharing their news and stories.

The Akan people, who originally lived in the African Gold Coast region where Ghana is today, had a god who was a supreme storyteller. In fact, he owned all the stories in existence and his name was Anansi.

Anansi was a trickster (a perfect aspect for a storyteller) and often took the form of a spider, sometimes with a man's face and sometimes in a man's body. Anansi was able to spin a web of delight and imagination to all he spoke with, but there was a time when there were no stories at all in the world and it was Anansi's cunning that brought them home.

The sky father, Nyame, had hidden all the stories in the world in a great box. Anansi found out about the box and wanted the world to hear the stories. He cast his web right up to where the sky father lived and asked him to open the box. Nyame didn't want to give up all the stories but thought it might be interesting to set this strange creature a series of impossible tasks to test his worth. If Anansi was successful in the tasks, then the stories would be his.

Anansi had to capture three of the most dangerous creatures in the world: Onini the python, Osebo the leopard and the frightening Mmoboro hornets. Through his courage, intelligence and with a good dose of trickery, Anansi managed to capture all three and Nyame gave up his story box. Not only were all the stories released to the spidery Anansi, but he was made the supreme god of stories so he too could live forever.

MORE EFFECTIVE COMMUNICATION SPELL

Every one of us can use a spell to help us be better communicators, whether that is in business or personal relationships or in our creative work. If you are a writer or someone who has to speak well professionally, this is a really powerful and useful spell to assist you.

You will need a white or yellow candle, some incense and a representation of Anansi; I do a simple little drawing of a spider or I do the spell near a spider's web. You'll be opening a circle for this so you can do this inside or outside. A waxing or full moon is the advantageous lunar energy.

Open your circle however you like, but a simple way is to place your energy in your feet, plug into the earth, breathe in and out a few times and bring the energy of the earth up through your body. Trace the circle with your outstretched hand, finger tracing the circle and saying: 'To the north, to the south, to the east, to the west, I am protected and am making great magic!'

LIGHT THE CANDLE AND SAY: *'Anansi, you who are the clever god of all stories, help me tell mine well. Bless me and protect me.'*

Describe out loud the blocks to good communication you might have: what is in the way, what normally happens when you don't communicate well or what isn't working. Use specific examples and be honest even though it may be hard to talk about. For example: you may not be able to speak up in meetings, you might get tongue tied with someone or you are afraid to speak your truth. Know that this is being received and transformed by Anansi.

SAY: *'Anansi, I seek a better way to speak my stories to go out into the world so they are sung. From now, show me how to speak authentically and to move forward wisely and fearlessly.'*

Light the incense and watch the smoke rise and carry effortlessly into the air just as your words will travel easily and quickly. Thank Anansi, close your circle and take one action, no matter how small, toward your intention.

SPRING

TIME TO BLOSSOM AND GROW

When you might be feeling stuck or that things aren't going the way you thought they would, I recommend turning your attention to what happens in spring. Every single year the cycle twists and flows until we get the big new fresh start!

Spring always proves to me that I will get a chance to try again, I will get a chance to grow, to change, to reach for something beyond what I have now. Spring gives me the opportunity to dream and to know that this dreaming can blossom into something real in time.

Like fall, spring is one of the shoulder seasons of transformation. It unwraps itself slowly but surely, which we catch sight of first in the returning of the light. Our day starts sooner, the birds begin singing earlier and for longer. The hard crust of the ground softens and small hopeful green shoots appear. Ice melts, as perhaps does our heart.

Many folk feel as though they want to open up their houses wide after being cocooned in winter. People begin to talk about decluttering and spring cleaning. Spring is also the perfect time for a 'spring clean' of old patterns and beliefs that you don't need to hold on to any more.

In the southern hemisphere, the Wheel of the Year turns and we celebrate the primary festival of fertility, Beltane, and the spring equinox of Ostara.

THE ULTIMATE SPRING SWEEP

I love making traditional clearing sweeps for my home. I make them seasonally so that the energies in my home are always fresh and flowful and my space protected. Here is an effective one for the spring season. Make some up ahead of time and leave it out under a dark or new moon for the highest effect.

You'll need 250 g of lightly crushed sea salt, a handful each of dried rosemary, wormwood, dried mint and dried rose petals or rose geranium leaves, a crystal that soaks up negative energy such as hematite, obsidian, smoky quartz or jet and your besom (broom) or a vacuum cleaner.

Place the sea salt and dried herbs/petals in a bowl and mix gently. Breathe good energy upon the mix as you stir. Place the crystal on the top. Leave the mixture out under a new or full moon for energising. Ensure no water can get in the bowl overnight.

When you are ready, toss pinches of the mixture in all of the rooms in your house, saying: 'Out, out, get it out! Nothing negative is about!' Leave for 10 minutes, then sweep or vacuum up the room thoroughly. Your rooms and house will feel very different! Go into each room and set a new intention for that space.

WHEEL OF THE YEAR:

Ostara

SPRING EQUINOX, 20-22 MARCH, 5.37 AM EDST

Ostara is the spring equinox, a time when we have perfect balance between the forces of dark and light. However, from the morrow light will increase day by day. Every day after Ostara the daylight hours and thus too the warmth and fertile energies of the land will build up until the big powerful energies of summer and Litha arrive.

Traditionally, Ostara was celebrated as a time of planting and growth. Our ancestors would certainly have been busy planting or tending the crop that was already begun. Animals born during Imbolc in early spring would be growing fast, and it would be a busy place on the farm.

Everything is expansive at this time and so should be your ideas and visions for yourself. The light is becoming more dominant, as should your feelings of stretching for the new. This is the time to take up a new challenge, learn something new, devise something fresh or take a risk that you have been thinking of taking for a while.

It is also about now that we begin to get that itch for a good spring clean out, which can mean you need to reduce clutter or to physically clean things up, but you can go deeper than that within yourself. This is the perfect time to think about what is keeping you heavy, for example, old beliefs or a grudge, and to let those things go. Remember: holding a grudge is like drinking poison and thinking the other person will die!

Ostara is a celebration of all the gifts the earth offers to us and how we can give back. This reciprocation to the earth is important now more than ever. We cannot continue to think of the planet as some kind of never-ending resource to be depleted and exploited; in fact, taking the word 'resource' out of the equation would be a great start. The basic gifts of the earth – water, clean air, good food – are under threat.

Ostara reminds us of the goodness and fertility we have. It reminds us that the earth gives us so much, including medicine. We are reminded too that we can reduce and change what isn't so good for us.

One of the most traditional symbols of Ostara is the egg. I paint them up and decorate my altar with them, and I like to perform rituals with them.

The other great thing to do for Ostara is to make a flower crown with all the fresh blossoms and herbs around. Make it as fragrant and as extravagant as you can, then wear it and hang it on your door or use it to decorate your altar.

1 Monday

Waning

Spring is here and it's time to make some changes! Simplify? A seasonal diet change? A spring clean?

2 Tuesday

Waning

3 Wednesday

Waning

4 Thursday

Waning

Thors-day was named after the Norse god Thor.

5 Friday

Waning

6 Saturday

Waning

7 Sunday

Waning

Binding spells are at their most powerful in the waning cycle. What negative behaviour would you like to bind?

Follow the breath inwards and outwards, for the motion is a good teacher.

– THE GODDESS

M	T	W	T	F	S	S
1	2	3	4	5	6	7
8	9	10	11	12	13	14
15	16	17	18	19	20	21
22	23	24	25	26	27	28
29	30	31				

8 Monday

Waning

9 Tuesday

Waning

10 Wednesday

Waning

11 Thursday

Waning

Harvest tuber or root vegetables at this time.

12 Friday

Dark moon

Let it go. Release gently but completely.

13 Saturday, ☽ new moon in Pisces, 5.21 am EDST

Dream big!

A wonderful night for making aqua luna (moon water). Leave the purest water you can find in a white or silver bowl under the moon and retrieve and bottle it prior to dawn. Use this in your spellcraft, your potions and even your bath!

14 Sunday ◑

Waxing

MARCH

M	T	W	T	F	S	S
	1	2	3	4	5	6	7
8	9	10	11	12	13	14
15	16	17	18	19	20	21
22	23	24	25	26	27	28
29	30	31				

15 Monday

Waxing

How are your new year's intentions faring?

16 Tuesday

Waxing

17 Wednesday

Waxing

18 Thursday

Waxing

19 Friday

Waxing

20 Saturday,  Ostara, spring equinox 5.37 am EDST

One of the most joyful festivals in the Wheel of the Year! The hours of night and day are equal, but from tomorrow the days grow longer. The warmth and light are returning to the earth day by day. A beautiful time of joy and balance. Set intentions for health and life balance.

21 Sunday

Waxing

Glorious is the world. The grain of sparkling sand is perfectly formed to the sentinel sequoia: observe.

– THE GODDESS

MARCH

M	T	W	T	F	S	S
1	2	3	4	5	6	7
8	9	10	11	12	13	14
15	**16**	**17**	**18**	**19**	**20**	**21**
22	23	24	25	26	27	28
29	30	31				

22 Monday

Waxing

23 Tuesday

Waxing

24 Wednesday

Waxing

25 Thursday

Waxing

26 Friday

Waxing

27 Saturday

Waxing

28 Sunday, ◯ full moon in Libra, 2.48 pm EDST

Extend your energy out into the world. This is an expansive time for you to use your energy intelligently.

MARCH

M	T	W	T	F	S	S
1	2	3	4	5	6	7
8	9	10	11	12	13	14
15	16	17	18	19	20	21
22	**23**	**24**	**25**	**26**	**27**	**28**
29	30	31				

APRIL

- ◆ What would I like to create, experience and manifest this month?

_____

_____

_____

_____

- ◆ What are the important dates for me this month?

_____

_____

- ◆ What would give me joy this month?

_____

_____

- ◆ What am I devoted to?

_____

_____

- ◆ Ideas, musings, actions:

_____

_____

_____

MAEVE

GODDESS OF THE MONTH: APRIL

I have to say I'm always a little bit taken with goddesses who seem to have a bad reputation, such as Circe, Hekate, Kali and our goddess of April, the Irish Maeve. Usually there is a big misunderstanding about the goddess and it normally goes through the filter of little systems such as patriarchy or other cultural straitjackets for women.

Maeve is a resplendently beautiful but also sharply intelligent warrior goddess. She was strategic, forceful and quite ruthless at times but she was always courageous and sought equality with any man she met. She is known as Medb, or she who intoxicates, due to the incredible personal power she wielded and the fact she was also the goddess of wine and mead.

Maeve was so beautiful that on the battlefield men would surrender at her feet in desire. All kinds of animals would follow her and birds would perch upon her shoulders. She could run faster than a mighty stallion, and her voice could be like the most gentle brook or like the roar of a violent storm.

Let me share one of the many stories of Maeve from the epic Táin Bó Cúailnge. Maeve and her consort husband King Ailil were lying in bed one lazy afternoon talking about and comparing their personal riches and possessions. Ailil wants to prove he is more powerful than Maeve in what he possesses, yet Maeve is able to match him evenly until Ailil mentions he owns a magnificent magical bull. This was very disturbing to Maeve, as she prided herself on being equal or superior to all men.

She is determined to find a magical bull and recalls there is such a beast in Cooley in the north. Maeve decides to capture the bull and prepares her army and her chariot. She takes to the battlefield and the enemy falls away at the sight of her. The hero Cuchulain resists her and manages to kill Queen Maeve's lovely handmaiden Locha, but Maeve eventually captures the bull.

The bull is put into a field with Ailil's bull. The bulls fight and kill each other, thus speaking resoundingly of the futility of war and bloodshed.

Courage spell

We all sometimes need a big dose of courage. It is okay to be fearful, as courage will help us move forward anyway.

Take a salt bath or shower to cleanse yourself. Dress impressively, for you will be meeting a queen.

RELAX AND LIGHT A GOLD CANDLE CANDLE AND SAY: *'Queen of the Connaught, Maeve, you who intoxicate. Queen! Warrior! I ask for your blessing and power. Raise your shield about me. I ask for your protection.'*

Shut your eyes and imagine Maeve and her chariot racing towards you. She stops, alights the chariot and smiles at you. You feel her power. Tell Maeve what your needs are and where you need courage. Tell her exactly what your fears are, really feeling them and offering them to her. Know that Maeve is powerful and she rewards the brave. Imagine her now placing her hand upon your heart and transferring her confident and courageous energy to you.

SAY: *'I am not afraid. You are with me, Maeve.'*

Stay in her embrace for as long as you need to; take your time.

Open your eyes and pick up a glass of mead or wine. Offer Maeve some by pouring it on the ground, saving the last sip for yourself. You are now in agreement.

Bow to Maeve and thank her, and blow out the candle.

Beltane (Bel Tan or Beltaine)

30 APRIL

Wild and full of love magic, Beltane demonstrates the intoxicating energy of life. It is the opposite on the Wheel of the Year to Samhain (Halloween), so where Samhain celebrates death and a void, Beltane is the embodiment of lusty life and super fertility.

Beltane translates literally into the words 'good fire', and our ancestors took the returning of warmth and lifeblood to the land literally by lighting massive torches right through the country. Feasts and ceremonies accompanied the fires and it was a time of joy and happiness.

Some of the earliest Beltane celebrations called for the May queen and king of the community to be united in ceremony. After ritual they would make love upon the earth to bring fertility to the soil. The community would also show their unity on their own land by wildly running, painting symbols upon their bodies, making music, drumming, telling stories and feasting.

The modern Beltane is still seen in May Day celebrations, when there is dancing around a maypole. The pole is usually wrapped in red and white ribbons and has young maidens dancing around it. The origins of these dances are fertility based, honouring the forces that bring seeding and growth back to the soil.

Again, as at Samhain, the veils between the worlds are at their thinnest so it is also one of the two best nights of the year to perform divination. Imagine our ancient and not-so-ancient ancestors scrying by fire, tossing runes or doing ogham wood readings.

If you are looking for the perfect energy to conceive a baby or an idea, here is your night!

To celebrate Beltane, I get up very early on Beltane morning and light a candle. With this flame I ask for the season's blessings and that fertility and happiness be upon my house. I clear and clean my altar and decorate it in white and red, including big bunches of fresh flowers and ripe fruits. I also light candles. I then do some divination such as with oracle cards and do a reading to ask for answers to any questions I might have.

As the energy of Beltane lends itself to potion making, it is on this day that I blend and make all kinds of healing salves and potions. I may also make some talismans for love, the healing of relationships and for conception and prosperity.

29 Monday

Waning

30 Tuesday

Waning

31 Wednesday

Waning

1 Thursday   April

Waning

April Fool's Day.

2 Friday

Waning

3 Saturday

Waning

4 Sunday

Waning

MARCH

M	T	W	T	F	S	S
1	2	3	4	5	6	7
8	9	10	11	12	13	14
15	16	17	18	19	20	21
22	23	24	25	26	27	28
29	**30**	**31**				

APRIL

M	T	W	T	F	S	S
			1	**2**	**3**	**4**
5	6	7	8	9	10	11
12	13	14	15	16	17	18
19	20	21	22	23	24	25
26	27	28	29	30		

5 Monday

Waning

6 Tuesday

Waning

7 Wednesday

Waning

8 Thursday

Waning

9 Friday

Waning

10 Saturday

Dark moon

11 Sunday, ☽ new moon in Aries, 10.30 pm EDST

Don't hold back! State powerfully where renewal needs to find its way into your life. The time for you is now.

The winds play upon your skin to tickle you into awakening.

– THE GODDESS

APRIL

M	T	W	T	F	S	S
			1	2	3	4
5	6	7	8	9	10	11
12	13	14	15	16	17	18
19	20	21	22	23	24	25
26	27	28	29	30		

12 Monday

Waxing

13 Tuesday

Waxing

14 Wednesday

Waxing

15 Thursday

Waxing

16 Friday

Waxing

17 Saturday

Waxing

18 Sunday

Waxing

APRIL

M	T	W	T	F	S	S
			1	2	3	4
5	6	7	8	9	10	11
12	13	14	15	16	17	18
19	20	21	22	23	24	25
26	27	28	29	30		

19 Monday

Waxing

20 Tuesday

Waxing

21 Wednesday

Waxing

22 Thursday

Waxing

23 Friday

Waxing

24 Saturday

Waxing

UN World Day for laboratory animals. Be conscious about products that have animal testing as part of their manufacture; you can choose cruelty free.

25 Sunday

Waxing

Rebel my beloved from all that keeps you crooked and small. Flowers raise their faces to the sun.

– THE GODDESS

APRIL						
M	T	W	T	F	S	S
			1	2	3	4
5	6	7	8	9	10	11
12	13	14	15	16	17	18
19	20	21	22	23	24	25
26	27	28	29	30		

26 Monday, ○ full moon in Scorpio, 11.31 pm EDST

Super full moon

A no-excuses big full moon! Lay down all your procrastination and set big intentions. Be courageous.

27 Tuesday ◑

Waning

28 Wednesday ◑

Waning

29 Thursday ◑

Waning

30 Friday

Waning

Happy Beltane! Celebrate the good (bel) fire (tan). Delight in the most fertile of spring energies and growth today and tonight. Allow yourself a little wildness and make merry. It's a magical night for lovers and lovemaking. Decorate your altar with fresh flowers or make a maypole.

1 Saturday   May

Waning

2 Sunday

Waning

	APRIL									MAY				
M	T	W	T	F	S	S		M	T	W	T	F	S	S
			1	2	3	4							1	2
5	6	7	8	9	10	11		3	4	5	6	7	8	9
12	13	14	15	16	17	18		10	11	12	13	14	15	16
19	20	21	22	23	24	25		17	18	19	20	21	22	23
26	27	28	29	30				24	25	26	27	28	29	30
								31						

MAY

- What would I like to create, experience and manifest this month?

_____

_____

_____

_____

- What are the important dates for me this month?

_____

_____

- What would give me joy this month?

_____

_____

- What am I devoted to?

_____

_____

- Ideas, musings, actions:

_____

_____

_____

CERRIDWEN

GODDESS OF THE MONTH: MAY

As we are still within fall, the energies of transformation remain strong. We are almost into the chills of winter, so it is the perfect time to begin to release what you no longer need and to lighten your load. The Welsh goddess Cerridwen, normally depicted stirring a great bubbling cauldron, invites you to change what you no longer need into something that you do.

If we think about the simple, alchemic process of cooking it gives us a good insight into her power. Let's say you are cooking a stew. You place many different ingredients into the cooking pot, but before you put them in they are simply what they are: carrots, potatoes, lentils and so on. However, when heated in the pot together with oil and water they no longer stay individual ingredients; they become, they transform, into something else: stew! It was said that Cerridwen's cauldron contained a potion of great power and could grant unlimited wisdom to those who drank of it. Anything that went into her pot was transformed and this is her great gift.

As we move into winter there is no need to carry the weight of burdens old and new; the wise crone aspect of Cerridwen invites you to place your worries, anxieties and fears into her pot. I think there is always something we may wish to place in the bubbling cauldron of transformation. For most of us there is a behaviour, fear, niggling worry or old pattern that we could do without. Here is your chance to offer it to Cerridwen, who will morph it into something way more useful for you.

I love to do these kinds of obstacle-reducing spells on a new or waxing moon, which are great times to let go and make room for something fresh.

CERRIDWEN'S CAULDRON SPELL

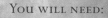

YOU WILL NEED:

- a brown or deep purple candle
- incense or burn pine resin on a charcoal
- strips of paper and a black pen
- a flameproof bowl or cooking pot

Ahead of time, do some serious thinking about what you would like transformed in your life; make a list if you like. Bring this with you to where you will perform the spell.

LIGHT THE CANDLE AND SAY: *'I have come here for change. I have come here to let things go that no longer serve me. I have come to be transformed!'*

LIGHT THE INCENSE OR RESIN AND CHARCOAL AND SAY: *'I invite you to assist me, Cerridwen. Place these things in your cauldron!'*

On each paper strip, write one thing you wish to get rid of.

AS YOU CATCH EACH ONE ON FIRE FROM YOUR CANDLE SAY OUT LOUD: *'I have an issue with ___ [state the thing you no longer need]. I release this to Cerridwen's cauldron. It no longer is!'*

Place the burning paper in your pot and allow all the strips to burn down to ashes.

ASK: *'Great goddess: is there anything I need to do so these never return?'* and listen for guidance. Don't think; listen! Act on any messages.

Blow out the candle with thanks and pour the ashes into your garden or on a plant.

3 Monday

Waning

4 Tuesday

Waning

Tuesday was named after Twia, the Celtic/Germanic god of war and the sky. The Norse god Tyr is also closely identified with this day.

5 Wednesday

Waning

6 Thursday

Waning

7 Friday

Waning

8 Saturday

Waning

9 Sunday

Waning

MAY

M	T	W	T	F	S	S
					1	2
3	4	5	6	7	8	9
10	11	12	13	14	15	16
17	18	19	20	21	22	23
24	25	26	27	28	29	30
31						

10 Monday

Dark moon

Rest and relax. Dream and gently plan.

11 Tuesday, new moon in Taurus, 2.59 pm EDST

Micro new moon

Set bright new intentions for your home or family. This is also a great time to ensure you are living as healthy a life as possible.

12 Wednesday

Waxing

13 Thursday

Waxing

14 Friday

Waxing

15 Saturday

Waxing

16 Sunday

Waxing

Rest and rejoice, for the darkness loves you as much as the light.
One is no better than the other.

– THE GODDESS

MAY

M	T	W	T	F	S	S
					1	2
3	4	5	6	7	8	9
10	11	12	13	14	15	16
17	18	19	20	21	22	23
24	25	26	27	28	29	30
31						

17 Monday ◐

Waxing

18 Tuesday ◐

Waxing

Plant seeds for plants that are above the underground growers such as basil and eggplant.

19 Wednesday ◐

Waxing

20 Thursday ◐

Waxing

21 Friday

Waxing

22 Saturday

Waxing

23 Sunday

Waxing

MAY

M	T	W	T	F	S	S
					1	2
3	4	5	6	7	8	9
10	11	12	13	14	15	16
17	**18**	**19**	**20**	**21**	**22**	**23**
24	25	26	27	28	29	30
31						

24 Monday

Waxing

25 Tuesday

Waxing

26 Wednesday, ◯ full moon in Sagittarius, 7.13 am EDST

Super full moon

A moon that encourages honesty, both yours and others. Be mindful of what you wish for as this expansive moon may give you what you need rather than what you want.

Penubral lunar eclipse visible in New York.

27 Thursday

Waning

28 Friday

Waning

29 Saturday

Waning

30 Sunday

Waning

MAY

M	T	W	T	F	S	S
					1	2
3	4	5	6	7	8	9
10	11	12	13	14	15	16
17	18	19	20	21	22	23
24	25	26	27	28	29	30
31						

JUNE

- What would I like to create, experience and manifest this month?

_____

_____

_____

_____

- What are the important dates for me this month?

_____

_____

- What would give me joy this month?

_____

_____

- What am I devoted to?

_____

_____

- Ideas, musings, actions:

_____

_____

_____

THE RAINBOW SERPENT

DEITY OF THE MONTH: JUNE

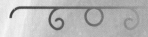

In Australia, the ancient creation myths of the first Australians featured the Rainbow Serpent. The serpent's story, whether oral or drawn, differs slightly from place to place yet always centres on the pivotal power of water. Water breathes life into the land and is central to growth, fertility and regeneration.

The name of the Rainbow Serpent is Goorialla or Nygalod or Borlung, depending on which tribe is speaking of him. Some believe the Rainbow Serpent brought water from heaven when the world was created. Others believe that in the beginning, when there was nothing on earth and the earth was flat, the Rainbow Serpent cracked through the crust of the earth and began his journey of waking up all life. As he moved and travelled, stopped and slept, with his body he created gullies and gorges, mountains and valleys and the water lines that joined them all. Once water appeared life on earth began to flourish; all the animals, reptiles and birds awoke and began their life cycles.

Australia is one of most environmentally sensitive places on the planet, our lack of water being but one reason for this. The Rainbow Serpent asks us to recognise the preciousness of water and how we rely upon it for the continuation of life. No matter where we live, water is vital for the health of our planet and ourselves and we can call upon the Rainbow Serpent to help.

In summer we feel the power of the sun and the lack of water, and also rain's great gift of rejuvenation when we do receive it. We drink, play, connect and float on the path of the great serpent's journey during December and have an opportunity to open our eyes more fully to the preciousness of water and how it delivers to us lifeblood and joy.

Seasonal summer meditation

You may want to honour the Rainbow Serpent by simply being mindful of the amount of water you use. You may even wish to donate to or work on a waterway regeneration scheme or to educate yourself about permaculture and gardening with less water, or choose to regularly meditate in gratitude to this mighty bringer of water! Here is one meditation you can try.

Sit somewhere quiet, preferably outdoors. Turn off your phone unless you have recorded this for yourself. If you like, light a candle or have a bowl of water to wash your hands in to start.

Close your eyes, breathe deeply and centre. Connect the bones you're sitting on or your feet with the earth. Imagine a dry desert-like environment with nothing living in it: just dust. Feel the dryness in your nostrils and mouth.

There begins a rumbling, a deep vibration, that is quiet at first. You feel it in your base chakra, then it travels upwards through your whole body, getting stronger and stronger. There is a whistling sound, like the wind. The barren landscape in your vision is suddenly disturbed by a great serpent cracking through the parched surface. It is magnificent and huge. Each of her scales glisten with colour as she rises to her full height. As she begins to lower herself to the earth and moves quickly forward, in her tracks a great canyon is formed.

Rippling out from this rises a mountain. You watch as water fills the canyons and every track the serpent makes. Trees and plant arise from the mud, growing wild and luxuriant. As she continues to snake her way through the land, the vibrations around her cause other animals to break free of the dust and fish swim in the billabongs and seas.

Everything smells moist and sweet: flowers bloom, birds sing, animals are everywhere. Imagine swimming in this newly created waterway, being blessed, energised and renewed. Breathe in the life, the joy! Think how different this feels. Experience the difference; connect with everything. Set forth your personal intentions now!

Thank the Rainbow Serpent for this gift of life and promise her that you will live with balance and respect for all she has created. Gift some of your energy to the earth and the Rainbow Serpent in any way you choose. When you open your eyes, look around you and know things are different. Go forth knowing this!

SUMMER

BIG, BRIGHT AND BEAUTIFUL

Summer is an extroverted season that's all about the light and the heat, the longer days and the beautiful weather that lures us outside to be social. Winter may well have been about reduction and introversion but hey, baby, the energy is back!

Look around and see the lushness and that nature is peaking and pumping. While summer is perhaps the season that Australia (where I am from) is most famous for – the beach, the outdoor lifestyle, the holiday season lining up with the great weather – no matter where you find yourself in summer you can feel the abundance of energy and the golden blessings of a celebratory time of year.

Summer energy is wild and big. This feeling we get of expansion is just a symptom of how much energy is rising from the earth herself. I think it's important to take the time to engage with some of that amazing energy and fill yourself up with it. Yes, we can understand that too much of anything is not really good for us, but it's vital that your body, mind and spirit gets refilled brightly. Sunshine is not just for plants!

All the delights of summer are sensual delights: the smell of jasmine on the breeze, the feeling of salt water on your skin, the explosion of a juicy summer fruit in your mouth, the sound of music at an outdoor concert, more flesh exposed to the sun. It enables you to remember why you have a body, so spells for health and vitality work particularly well at this time.

It's not just sunshine that is so fantastic in summer: it's the warmer nights that enable us to stay out later and commune with the lush darkness. My garden is alive on summer nights, and when sitting outside under the moon watching the possum parade, the fruit bats flying in, the owls out hunt and the critters I can't see but I can hear I feel the ease and joy of the season.

Midsummer magic and mischief

Are you ready to play with the Fae?

The night before Litha (the longest night of the year) our ancestors would be travelling to special sites to celebrate the solstice. On the way through they had to pay particular attention to where they were going because the Fae were very active on this night, and they could sweep a person away.

The Fae were particularly mischievous and could play tricks if you didn't respect them. These could involve doing you out of your food or money or simply making you forget who and where you were. Midsummer's eve had all the excitement of travelling to one of the biggest festivals of the year laced with a little danger and wildness. It was customary to involve the Fae in celebrations on this eve so our little friends stayed our friends! There are lots of ways to do this and many of them can involve your children, as children love to try to sight faeries in the garden.

The traditional thing is to make up little food gifts for the Fae. I have a lot of pretty little plates, tiny ones that you might pour soy sauce into, and I add strawberries and cream and a bit of fresh honey from my hives. I place these wherever I think the Fae might see them or near places I think they might be, such as holes in a tree trunk, where mushrooms grow or fragrant flowers are richest. I also like to make up a couple of small baskets of berries and biscuits that I hang from the branches of trees. I add trailing ribbons in bright colours to catch the wind and the eye of the Fae!

I even leave notes to them on tiny bits of paper with very small writing telling them how happy I am to share a garden with them and how I love them to be there. I add a dash of glitter or some pretty crystals to all of this and I always feel particularly happy afterwards.

And another small thing: I set my intentions for my own wildness and freedom upon this night. Breathe and centre, smile and know that mischief hasn't left you. Enjoy!

WHEEL OF THE YEAR

✦

Litha

SUMMER SOLSTICE, 20-23 JUNE, 11.32 PM EDST

If there was a festival that asked for your authentic presence right now, this minute, to show up and be it is Litha. Litha is a solstice festival that celebrates the longest day and the shortest night of the year. It is about the peak of seasonal energy. Imagine our ancestors working the land and marking this time because, from then on, the days began to grow shorter, which was a reminder of how much time they had to grow and prepare all the foods they needed for harvest before the black of winter hit again.

The powerful energy of the now encourages us to fully experience and plug in to the wonderful energy that is on offer. Litha reminds us that we are enough, that our lives are full and a rich tapestry if we allow them to be. It is certainly a day for reciprocity and gratitude.

We also celebrate our bodies on such a day and our health as we experience it. If you are able to love your body and give it the best you can you will experience life even more fully, you will get to see more and do more.

Litha is traditionally a social festival so group rituals are particularly powerful. It embodies the idea of encouraging each other to do more and do things you really want to do rather than what you might see as a duty, to stand before your friends and set forth big goals for your future. This is a life-affirming act, and to be able to state what has come to fruition since last year is wonderful for your confidence.

As this day is also the day when the masculine energies are said to be at their strongest and are traditionally honoured, I like to do a devotional to the masculine divine in all its forms, especially the patrons I work with. I decorate my altar in orange, red and gold and place gifts for the deities I like to work with. The best time to do this is around midday.

Aqua sol (sun water) can be made successfully today; it's useful in potions and spells for your health and vitality and also for protection of the home. Aqua sol is made by leaving out a bowl of water for an hour or two from midday.

As this is the longest day, I like to see the sun go down and celebrate it. The ideal way is to get together with your buddies and have a dinner picnic and ritual. Afterwards, my friends and I bless coins under the sun and randomly leave them out as Litha gifts as a kind of fun reciprocity.

JUNE

31 Monday 🌓 May

Waning

1 Tuesday 🌓 June

Waning

A good day to trim your hair if you want it to keep it in a similar style.

2 Wednesday 🌓

Waning

3 Thursday 🌓

Waning

4 Friday

Waning

5 Saturday

Waning

6 Sunday

Waning

No matter how dark the night, you carry
the light within yourself.

– THE GODDESS

		MAY							JUNE				
M	T	W	T	F	S	S		M	T	W	T	F	S	S
					1	2		**1**	**2**	**3**	**4**	**5**	**6**
3	4	5	6	7	8	9		7	8	9	10	11	12	13
10	11	12	13	14	15	16		14	15	16	17	18	19	20
17	18	19	20	21	22	23		21	22	23	24	25	26	27
24	25	26	27	28	29	30		28	29	30				
31													

7 Monday

Waning

8 Tuesday

Waning

9 Wednesday

Dark moon

Listen to your own heartbeat. Go inwards and listen to the wisdom of your body.

10 Thursday, new moon in Gemini, 6.52 am EDST

Set intentions to better your communication with others and to refresh your attitude towards old grudges. Grudges are heavy; why carry them any longer?

11 Friday ◑

Waxing

12 Saturday ◑

Waxing

13 Sunday ◑

Waxing

JUNE

M	T	W	T	F	S	S
	1	2	3	4	5	6
7	**8**	**9**	**10**	**11**	**12**	**13**
14	15	16	17	18	19	20
21	22	23	24	25	26	27
28	29	30				

14 Monday

Waxing

15 Tuesday

Waxing

16 Wednesday

Waxing

17 Thursday

Waxing

18 Friday

Waxing

19 Saturday

Waxing

Midsummer's eve: a night of delicious joy and mischief! Watch out for the Fae in your garden or your favourite green space. A great night for divination and fun with your children. Traditional gifts of strawberries, honey and milk are left out in the wild places for the local Fae. I even add tiny stars to really attract them.

20 Sunday, 🌓 Litha, summer solstice, 11.32 pm EDST

Waxing

This is the day to honour the masculine divine in all its forms and celebrate the year's biggest festival of the sun. Rise at dawn, light a candle and catch as much energy as you can; it's the longest day of the year, after all!

Listen.
Find stillness like a rock in a river.

– THE GODDESS

JUNE

M	T	W	T	F	S	S
		1	2	3	4	5	6
7	8	9	10	11	12	13
14	**15**	**16**	**17**	**18**	**19**	**20**
21	22	23	24	25	26	27
28	29	30				

21 Monday

Waxing

22 Tuesday

Waxing

23 Wednesday

Waxing

24 Thursday, ○ full moon in Capricorn, 2.39 pm EDST

A moon to set intentions for your further education or to use logic and your heart to solve a situation.

25 Friday

Waning

26 Saturday

Waning

27 Sunday

Waning

Follow the breath inwards and outwards, for the motion is a good teacher.

– THE GODDESS

JUNE

M	T	W	T	F	S	S
	1	2	3	4	5	6
7	8	9	10	11	12	13
14	15	16	17	18	19	20
21	**22**	**23**	**24**	**25**	**26**	**27**
28	29	30				

JULY

◆ What would I like to create, experience and manifest this month?

_____

_____

_____

_____

◆ What are the important dates for me this month?

_____

_____

◆ What would give me joy this month?

_____

_____

◆ What am I devoted to?

_____

_____

◆ Ideas, musings, actions:

_____

_____

_____

NUIT

GODDESS OF THE MONTH: JULY

As we enter into the shorter days and longer nights, I find it an apt time to work with a deity that is considered 'dark'. The idea of 'dark' can scare some folks, but we need darkness as well as light, shadows as well as sunshine. If people are wary at first I always like to recommend a goddess such as Nuit.

Within the Egyptian pantheon, Nuit played the role of a sky goddess. While the celestial heavens were her body, below in a mirror image was her brother, the earth god Geb. Nuit's energy is as wide as the sky, as big as the universe and as bright as a star. The infinite sky and sparkling stars were expressions of the nature of Nuit. We only need to look up on a clear night sky to feel a strong feeling of wonder, unlimited possibility, infinity and perpetual life.

Nuit was also a goddess of death, albeit a loving motherly one. It was her energy the Egyptians believed their dead lovingly rested within, and her beautiful image was often painted on the lids of sarcophagi. It is no surprise to learn that she was also of assistance to sleepers.

Nuit sired the powerful deities Isis, Osiris, Set and Ra. The sun god was born each day from her star-strewn body and then swallowed up again at sunset.

Sometimes we feel stuck or small, at which time Nuit is a great ally. She invites you to understand deeply that you are part of the infinite and therefore full of possibility and expansiveness. She reminds you that you can set big goals or intentions, take a risk and fearlessly expand and open your mind. Nuit is also encouraging to those who feel they need to have all the answers all the time, which is exhausting on so many levels. Having some mystery in your life (and in your world) is quite magical and sacred.

FEARLESS EXPANSION WITH NUIT

I love to cast this spell during a full moon, but any clear night sky will do. Ahead of time, think about precisely where you need expansion: in your thinking, your heart or your purpose or career. You'll need to be dressed in dark or silver-coloured clothing and have handy a silver candle and incense (myrrh or frankincense is ideal).

LIGHT THE CANDLE AND SAY: *'Nuit of the night sky, fill me with wonder. Be with me now.'*

Lie or sit down, relax and breathe. Look at the night sky and the stars if you are outside; if not, just shut your eyes. Be aware of the places your body touches the earth or floor. Relax even more deeply into those places.

Place your attention on seeing the night sky either in reality or in your mind, those many, many tiny sparkling pinpricks of light that are stars. They are so beautiful, magnificent, open.

Look at yourself lying or sitting down. See yourself fully in great detail as if you are flying above, and look with love. See the room, see your house. See the outside of your house, the garden, the street, the area in which you live. Expand your view ever outwards until you can see the curve of the horizon.

Notice how big and wide everything is. See how free you feel? Look up at the universe: how wide and deep and mysterious it is. Notice that you are still relaxed and floating, light and carefree. Notice there are so many possibilities within such a huge expansiveness, so much you can do!

Float over to one of the stars and see it glittering like a giant diamond or crystal. As you float closer, see the face of Nuit in the star. She is smiling. She says to you: 'You are a unique star in an infinite universe and there is nothing to fear in your own expansion.' Tell her in what ways you would like to be more connected and fearless in your growth.

She nods and grants you your wish, and gives you a symbol of your larger, higher self. Know that you will find use for this later. Thank Nuit and allow yourself to feel the new expansiveness you have, the feeling that possibilities for you are endless and all will be well.

Travel back through your street, home or room until you see and merge with yourself again. Come back to the room.

SAY: *'I honour you, Nuit, great goddess of the infinite.'*

You might wish to ground yourself by eating or drinking something, having a bath or shower or listening to music with a strong beat.

28 Monday

Waning

29 Tuesday

Waning

30 Wednesday

Waning

End of the financial year. Consider how you would like to improve your finances next year.

1 Thursday

Waning

2 Friday

Waning

3 Saturday

Waning

Saturday was named after the Roman god Saturn.

4 Sunday

Waning

Flowers don't fly to bees.

- THE GODDESS

		JUNE				
M	**T**	**W**	**T**	**F**	**S**	**S**
	1	2	3	4	5	6
7	8	9	10	11	12	13
14	15	16	17	18	19	20
21	22	23	24	25	26	27
28	**29**	**30**				

		JULY				
M	**T**	**W**	**T**	**F**	**S**	**S**
			1	**2**	**3**	**4**
5	6	7	8	9	10	11
12	13	14	15	16	17	18
19	20	21	22	23	24	25
26	27	28	29	30	31	

5 Monday

Waning

Harvest below-ground vegetables this week.

6 Tuesday

Waning

7 Wednesday

Waning

8 Thursday

Dark moon

This is a perfect night to do some shadow work and rid yourself of a bad habit or an old outdated belief.

9 Friday, new moon in Cancer, 9.16 pm EDST

Know that you can always begin again; we live in cycles, not linear lines. Set intentions for forgiveness and deep healing.

10 Saturday

Waxing

11 Sunday

Waxing

JULY

M	T	W	T	F	S	S
			1	2	3	4
5	6	7	8	9	10	11
12	13	14	15	16	17	18
19	20	21	22	23	24	25
26	27	28	29	30	31	

12 Monday

Waxing

13 Tuesday

Waxing

14 Wednesday

Waxing

15 Thursday

Waxing

16 Friday

Waxing

17 Saturday

Waxing

18 Sunday

Waxing

Develop stillness.

Be as the river stone surrounded by a raging river.

- THE GODDESS

JULY

M	T	W	T	F	S	S
			1	2	3	4
5	6	7	8	9	10	11
12	**13**	**14**	**15**	**16**	**17**	**18**
19	20	21	22	23	24	25
26	27	28	29	30	31	

19 Monday

Waxing

20 Tuesday

Waxing

21 Wednesday

Waxing

22 Thursday

Waxing

23 Friday, ○ full moon in Aquarius, 10.36 pm EDST

Big change is what this moon is asking you for. Don't live small with this energy flowing around you.

24 Saturday ◗

Waning

25 Sunday ◗

Waning

JULY

M	T	W	T	F	S	S
			1	2	3	4
5	6	7	8	9	10	11
12	13	14	15	16	17	18
19	**20**	**21**	**22**	**23**	**24**	**25**
26	27	28	29	30	31	

26 Monday

Waning

27 Tuesday

Waning

28 Wednesday

Waning

29 Thursday

Waning

30 Friday

Waning

31 Saturday

Waning

1 Sunday, Lammas   August

Waning

Lammas: the traditional time of first harvest and a time of gratitude. Express your gratitude for the harvest of your life so far.

Blossom and unfurl; this is your birthright. Golden and soft, dark and resilient.

- THE GODDESS

		JULY				
M	T	W	T	F	S	S
			1	2	3	4
5	6	7	8	9	10	11
12	13	14	15	16	17	18
19	20	21	22	23	24	25
26	**27**	**28**	**29**	**30**	**31**	

		AUGUST				
M	T	W	T	F	S	S
						1
2	3	4	5	6	7	8
9	10	11	12	13	14	15
16	17	18	19	20	21	22
23	24	25	26	27	28	29
30	31					

AUGUST

- ◆ What would I like to create, experience and manifest this month?

_____

_____

_____

_____

- ◆ What are the important dates for me this month?

_____

_____

- ◆ What would give me joy this month?

_____

_____

- ◆ What am I devoted to?

_____

_____

- ◆ Ideas, musings, actions:

_____

_____

_____

ARTIO

GODDESS OF THE MONTH: AUGUST

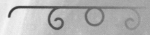

Humans have been honouring bear deities since Paleolithic times, and we know Neanderthals took part in bear cults. Bears worldwide are a symbol of protection, power and nature herself.

Bears are strong and powerful creatures. Their behaviour of standing up on their hind legs gives them human likeness, and many cultures saw them as transformational creatures that embodied the spirit of their ancestors or friends. Particularly resonant with power are she-bears because of the way they protect their young against all dangers, yet they are tender and loving towards those they care for.

The ancient Celts, Gauls and peoples of the far north certainly had a number of bear deities. One was Artio, the she-bear. Artio (artos means bear in Celtic) could take both a human female form and that of a giant she-bear. She was a protectress of wild places and the animals that lived within them, and was a symbol of the land's fertility and women's power.

There is a particularly exquisite statue of Artio in Sweden that was originally part of an ancient Roman temple estate. The bronze shows an extremely realistic portrait of Artio as a bear and another figure facing Artio as the goddess in human form. We see the symbols of the trees of the forest, baskets of plenty and flowers and the strong connection between woman and bear. We know from this single statue that the cult of Artio survived the Roman invasion and period.

Protection for your animal companion

This is a protective spell working with Artio for the protection of your beautiful animal companions. We transform your animal items into a protective amulet of sorts, and it's a lovely spell to cast.

Ahead of time, make some aqua luna (water left out under a full moon) for use in this spell. You'll also need a white or green candle, an offering of honey for Artio and something belonging to your companion such as a collar, tags, lead or a pet bed. Go outside for this spell and have everything close at hand.

Light the candle and say: *'Blessed Artio, great she-bear, I come before you today to ask you for your blessings and protection upon my animal companion _____* [name them here]. *I love them dearly and I would like them protected and watched over. I have an offering for you, Artio.'* (Pour a little honey on the ground.)

Hold the bowl of water and close your eyes. Imagine being in the green forest and open all your senses to this. See Artio in her flower-bedecked human form coming towards you, blessing the water in your hands. Feel her love and protection. Thank Artio for her presence and blessing.

Open your eyes and put your hand into the water, lifting a little of it out and flicking it upon the belongings of your animal companion.

Say: *'In the name of Artio I bless this _____* [name the item]. *May it protect my companion and may they enjoy this peacefully, joyfully and in good health.'*

Blow out the candle and give your animal its new blessed gift.

WHEEL OF THE YEAR:

Lammas

Imagine a festival where you get to sit down after a load of hard work and celebrate the bounty you have produced. You get to feast and dance and be grateful with everyone else. This is the festival of Lammas.

Our ancestors, who produced everything themselves from butter to growing all their own food, celebrated Lammas as a harvest festival, giving thanks for the bounty of what they had produced. Nature was honoured too for the fertility of what she herself provided, and this reciprocity was returned by honouring the land and the deities that were so generous.

We know that Lammas was a social festival shared among the community, so the connective energy was something tightly felt. Coming together to express gratitude for the harvest was a decidedly positive practice that had many ongoing benefits.

Feeling active gratitude for what we have is something we all should consider doing on a regular basis: understanding what we have, how far we have come, how we have grown and what we have been able to do better. True gratitude is transformational.

I always start celebrating Lammas by decorating my altar and baking. An altar is something that should never be left stagnant; it should change and evolve as the cycles do. A Lammas altar could feature all the colours of a harvest: orange, brown and gold. My altar always features a big plate of food, including baked goods such as bread and cakes.

I'm not a particularly great cook, but this doesn't matter. Every year I get up early on Lammas and bake bread and I try to include ingredients that I have harvested in my garden such as herbs. If I don't have time to bake a cake I might buy cupcakes of many colours, which always look wonderful on a Lammas feast table. Additionally, I plan a feast with friends to which everyone brings a plate. The emphasis is on lovingly home-cooked meals using seasonal produce.

Candles are lit and everyone speaks about what they are grateful for and what their personal harvest is for this time. It's a good idea to think about your greatest achievements to share in advance because sometimes it's hard to think about these in the moment. Marking the progress or success in our hard work is important; too often we find ourselves on a treadmill where we don't stop to see how far we have actually come. Sharing this harvest with those we love and getting some support helps us remember we can and do make progress when we feel stuck.

2 Monday ◑

Waning

3 Tuesday ◑

Waning

4 Wednesday ◑

Waning

5 Thursday ◑

Waning

6 Friday

Waning

7 Saturday

Dark moon

Joyfully let go; nothing negative to keep here.

8 Sunday,) new moon in Leo, 9.50 am EDST

An powerfully action-orientated new moon. Mean what you say; deliver on the promises you make to yourself.

Allow the blood rush of nature warm your soul, flood your mind
and revive your spirit.

- THE GODDESS

AUGUST						
M	T	W	T	F	S	S
2	3	4	5	6	7	8
9	10	11	12	13	14	15
16	17	18	19	20	21	22
23	24	25	26	27	28	29
30	31					

9 Monday

Waxing

10 Tuesday

Waxing

11 Wednesday

Waxing

12 Thursday

Waxing

13 Friday

Waxing

14 Saturday

Waxing

15 Sunday

Waxing

AUGUST						
M	T	W	T	F	S	S
2	3	4	5	6	7	8
9	**10**	**11**	**12**	**13**	**14**	**15**
16	17	18	19	20	21	22
23	24	25	26	27	28	29
30	31					

16 Monday

Waxing

17 Tuesday

Waxing

18 Wednesday

Waxing

19 Thursday

Waxing

20 Friday ◑

Waxing

21 Saturday ◑

Waxing

22 Sunday, ○ full moon in Aquarius, 8.01 am EDST

Blue moon

Think big! A moon for making big wishes for the healing and advancement of the whole of the earth.

M	T	W	T	F	S	S
	2	3	4	5	6	7	8
9	10	11	12	13	14	15
16	17	18	19	20	21	22
23	24	25	26	27	28	29
30	31					

23 Monday ☽

Waning

24 Tuesday ☽

Waning

25 Wednesday ☽

Waning

26 Thursday ☽

Waning

27 Friday

Waning

28 Saturday

Waning

Fall is here, change is afoot.

29 Sunday

Waning

AUGUST

M	T	W	T	F	S	S
2	3	4	5	6	7	8
9	10	11	12	13	14	15
16	17	18	19	20	21	22
23	24	25	26	27	28	29
30	31					

SEPTEMBER

♦ What would I like to create, experience and manifest this month?

_____

_____

_____

_____

♦ What are the important dates for me this month?

_____

_____

♦ What would give me joy this month?

_____

_____

♦ What am I devoted to?

_____

_____

♦ Ideas, musings, actions:

_____

_____

_____

POSEIDON

GOD OF THE MONTH: SEPTEMBER

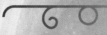

As gentle as a lagoon and as destructive as a tsunami, Poseidon was one of the greatest gods of the Greek pantheon. One of the sons of Cronus (time), he ruled the sea. His brothers Zeus and Hades ruled the sky and the underworld respectively.

Although loving and fearing him at the same time, sailors in the ancient world would often make sacrifices to Poseidon before any voyage for their safety, and fishermen would partake in great seasonal rites to appease him. Some rites were as straightforward as singing to him in a storm as the swells grew; some were simple such as tracing his trident upon the shore before entering the sea; and some were blood sacrifices of horses so he could enjoy a new mount for his chariot, a ritual undertaken by Alexander the Great.

In his aspect as a god of fertility, like Zeus, we see Poseidon as a highly virile figure chasing the feminine divine all over, with his couplings resulting in many children including Pegasus, the magnificent winged horse. Surfers, sailors, fishermen and anyone who has a deep love and appreciation of the water element would do well to regularly communicate with Poseidon. The essential aspect of water is its flow, which Poseidon controls with great power. Call upon him when you need a flow of anything in your life, but in particular creativity, fertility or prosperity.

I cannot expect Poseidon would be pleased with humans right now, as we have treated his realm like a garbage dump. We have caused many imbalances in our oceans from things such as overfishing and pollution. We need to call upon Poseidon for his help in protecting this domain and actively stop using so many plastics that end up in the oceans.

FLOWFUL SPELL FOR PROSPERITY

It used to be said in the ancient Greek world that if you wanted to be rich it was 'good to be as rich as Poseidon'. Here is a spell that helps with the flow of prosperity of all kinds.

Think about where you want prosperous flow within your life ahead of time, for example, better cash flow, more clients, a pay increase and so on. This is best done at a beach during an incoming tide or high tide.

STAND AT THE WATER'S EDGE. DRAW A TRIDENT SHAPE IN THE SAND WITH YOUR FINGER, FACE THE OCEAN AND CALL OUT: *'Mighty Poseidon, earth shaker, protector of the sea, tamer of horses and saviour of ships: hear my prayer! You who are responsible for the prosperity of trade and the flow of money, help me attract _____ [state here your intentions for your business, cash flow or new job, or where you feel the money will come from].'*

Speak well and truthfully. Offer a small single coin to the sand or waves.

As the water claims the trident in the sand, so has Poseidon heard your desire.

SAY: *'I go with your flow!'*

Thank Poseidon. You may also like to thank him by taking care of the ocean and beach environment somehow, such as taking rubbish away with you or making a donation to a cause that assists the oceans.

FALL

Nothing stays the same for long, and now we are in one of the seasons of transformation: fall (spring is the other season that, along with fall, demonstrate this the most).

Where I live, fall announces itself with colder mornings and winds that begin to blow from a different direction. The stifling heat that was previously unbroken is released just that little bit, so that the middle of the day isn't so punishing any more. We have new birds in my garden and my summer feathered friends are flying to other places

The wild growth of plants of the last few months ceases and everything begins to retreat.

The earth itself begins to stop its relentless growth and striving. Plants begin to come to final harvest and then settle back, with some dying away completely. It is at this time that we can take advantage of the powerful energy flow of change.

Change should never be resisted, as it is like standing in front of a big wave coming towards you at the beach. Turn and ride it in or get smashed by it!

I find fall the perfect time to bring change to aspects of my life that perhaps are not the way I would prefer them to be. I can tweak the things I do for my health, look more to my self-care, spend more time with my family and let go of worrying about things I have no control over (and that list is really loooong!). I might also change my business strategies or plan something completely new. All of these changes refine what I want more of.

To be able to purposely direct change at a time like this is something that will boost your confidence and empowerment.

HAPPY TRANSFORMATION SPELL

This is a wonderful spell to perform with your friends
and can be cast at any time of the lunar phase.

Decorate a table or your altar with fall colours and three orange or
gold candles. Ask your friends to bring along something that represents
transformation to them. Traditional symbols include fresh apples, leaves
that are turning colour, seeds or grain, empty cicada shells or anything
that is significantly changeable. Place these on the table or altar.

Ahead of time, all participants should think carefully about
exactly where they want transformation and change in their life.
Be specific, and take your time to work this through.

Cast a circle or simply welcome the positive energies of the universe
or your preferred deity into your space. Light the central candle and
ay out loud: 'We are gathered here in joy and hope and we thank the
universe and the energies of the planet for this blessing that we can all
be here together to share intentions. I call upon the powerful elements
of change as fall rolls forward. I call upon the winds, the cooling air and
the magic of transformation to take us from one state to another.'

Each person should in turn hold up their symbol of transformation. They
should mention why this offering means change to them, then they should
express where they seek change in the presence and support of the group.

After each person expresses this, everyone should say: 'I
lend you my energy. May this be so!' Light the second candle
and say: 'We trust that all will be as we have asked.'

Another person should light the third candle and say: 'This
is a symbol of our willingness to act and to accept change.'

Thank all the energies that have assisted you.
Let the candles burn down safely and leave the symbols
on your altar for a time.

WHEEL OF THE YEAR:

Mabon

FALL EQUINOX, 21-22 SEPTEMBER, 3.21 PM EDST

When I first came on this path, the festival of the Wheel of the Year that I began with was Mabon. It was perhaps not the most exciting of festivals to begin with; after all, Samhain seems a lot more fun! However underrated it might seem, Mabon is the first of the year's equinoxes, the times when the hours of light and dark in a day are equal. It is a powerful time.

I remember how incredibly busy I was as a young woman back then, with little time for myself or anything that I really wanted to do. I was giving out all the time and rarely taking in anything for myself. As an equinox Mabon teaches us about the importance of balance, so what this festival had to teach me was very apt for my circumstances. Learning how to find balance, true balance, within myself, my work and my relationships was life changing.

Mabon is the last harvest festival, which meant for those who worked on the land that winter was coming and this would be the last chance to harvest and prepare for a leaner time. And this harvest was a big one, the one that would have to be saved to feed folks through hard times. It could very well have been the difference between survival and perishing. The preparation and preservation of the bounty harvested was at the heart of the community.

This equinox would see the whole community coming together to make the best use of that harvest. Imagine the smoke houses smoking meats and fish, huge cauldrons of tomatoes and fruit being made into pastes and jellies, the cheeses and butters being churned and created; it was a busy and exciting time.

There is nothing like a big feast to celebrate Mabon or to do what our ancestors would have done and get together to produce lots of goodies that could be kept throughout the winter. Traditional feasting games included apple bobs and bake contests. Jams, pickles and jellies are brilliant to cook up with friends, as sharing the last harvests from your garden with others is so rewarding. For those of you with bees, this is the time for the last hive checks before winter.

My Mabon altar is always a big and robust one. I feature freshly baked bread, nuts and seasonal fruits. Another lovely idea is to bake cookies with one half a dark colour and one half light, symbolising the balance of the elements at this time. The colours featured are bronzes, golds and rich browns.

Mabon is also a perfect time to quietly assess whether or not your life is balanced. Where is it unbalanced, where can you do better? Where can you simplify? Where can you ramp it up or take some time out for solitude? By asking yourself robust questions like these and supplying honest answers, you can choose to change what you don't like, you can choose differently.

30 Monday ◑ August

Waning

31 Tuesday ◑

Waning

1 Wednesday ◑ September

Waning
First official day of fall.

2 Thursday ◑

Waning

3 Friday

Waning

4 Saturday

Waning

5 Sunday

Dark moon

Embrace the stillness and quiet of the full moon; it's a wonderful night to do binding spells.

Do not lose the physicality of your body; remember what each and every muscle does.

– THE GODDESS

AUGUST						
M	T	W	T	F	S	S
2	3	4	5	6	7	8
9	10	11	12	13	14	15
16	17	18	19	20	21	22
23	24	25	26	27	28	29
30	31					

SEPTEMBER						
M	T	W	T	F	S	S
		1	2	3	4	5
6	7	8	9	10	11	12
13	14	15	16	17	18	19
20	21	22	23	24	25	26
27	28	29	30			

6 Monday, new moon, Virgo, 8.51 pm EDST

A moon to set intentions of honesty, ethics and moving forward in clarity and joy.

7 Tuesday

Waxing

8 Wednesday

Waxing

9 Thursday

Waxing

10 Friday ◑

Waxing

11 Saturday ◑

Waxing

12 Sunday ◑

Waxing

Movement is stillness.

– THE GODDESS

SEPTEMBER

M	T	W	T	F	S	S
		1	2	3	4	5
6	**7**	**8**	**9**	**10**	**11**	**12**
13	14	15	16	17	18	19
20	21	22	23	24	25	26
27	28	29	30			

13 Monday

Waxing

14 Tuesday

Waxing

15 Wednesday

Waxing

16 Thursday

Waxing

17 Friday

Waxing

18 Saturday

Waxing

19 Sunday

Waxing

Crackle with the electricity you have running through
your veins.

– THE GODDESS

SEPTEMBER

M	T	W	T	F	S	S
		1	2	3	4	5
6	7	8	9	10	11	12
13	**14**	**15**	**16**	**17**	**18**	**19**
20	21	22	23	24	25	26
27	28	29	30			

20 Monday, ◯ full moon in Pisces, 7.54 pm EDST

Choose peace. A perfect moon to set intentions for harmony and peaceful resolutions to problems.

21 Tuesday

Waning

22 Wednesday, Mabon, fall equinox, 3.21 pm, EDST

Waning

Recognise the harvest of your life. Be grateful for what you have. Take stock of what has served you and what has not. Let go of what you no longer need and decide to change for the better.

23 Thursday

Waning

24 Friday

Waning

25 Saturday

Waning

A good day to remove any unwanted hair, as it will grow back more slowly.

26 Sunday

Waning

You are ALIVE.

- THE GODDESS

SEPTEMBER						
M	T	W	T	F	S	S
			1	2	3	4	5
6	7	8	9	10	11	12
13	14	15	16	17	18	19
20	**21**	**22**	**23**	**24**	**25**	**26**
27	28	29	30			

27 Monday

Waning

28 Tuesday

Waning

29 Wednesday

Waning

30 Thursday

Waning

1 Friday ◗

Waning

October

2 Saturday ◗

Waning

3 Sunday ◗

Waning

SEPTEMBER							OCTOBER						
M	T	W	T	F	S	S	M	T	W	T	F	S	S
	1	2	3	4	5						1	2	3
6	7	8	9	10	11	12	4	5	6	7	8	9	10
13	14	15	16	17	18	19	11	12	13	14	15	16	17
20	21	22	23	24	25	26	18	19	20	21	22	23	24
27	**28**	**29**	**30**				25	26	27	28	29	30	31

OCTOBER

- ◆ What would I like to create, experience and manifest this month?

_____

_____

_____

_____

- ◆ What are the important dates for me this month?

_____

_____

- ◆ What would give me joy this month?

_____

_____

- ◆ What am I devoted to?

_____

_____

- ◆ Ideas, musings, actions:

_____

_____

_____

OURANOS

GOD OF THE MONTH: OCTOBER

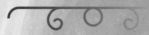

Almost every culture has creation myths, with the ancient Greeks being no exception. In the beginning there has been nothing but a primordial sludge, a full nothingness. This state was called Chaos. There then formed some organising influences that stepped from Chaos, the first of which were Eros (love) and Gaia (earth).

Because love in the form of Eros existed alongside her, Gaia gave self-birth to Ouranos/Uranus, the universe or the sky. She considered Ouranos her equal and they become joined. Ouranos explodes in joy and love, showering Gaia with stars and rain, and Gaia begets other gods, goddesses and Titans. The Titans born from Ouranos and Gaia were Oceanus, Coeus, Crius, Hyperion, Iapetus, Theia, Rhea, Phoebe, Tethys, Mnemosyne and Cronus. As each one was born Ouranos felt fear of them and cast them into the depths of earth in a Tartarus volcano.

This legend depicts the archetypal mother and father, with Ouranos being the masculine force and the fertile half of reproduction. Many ancient stories depict a repeated pattern of the masculine fearing being usurped by the children, especially the sons Ouranos was convinced would do him harm.

Gaia was pained by Ouranos' imprisonment of her sons and decided he had to be stopped. She created a sharp flint sickle and encouraged the Titans to seek revenge and their freedom, but only Cronus was willing to try. Cronus, who was ambitious and wished to be as powerful as his father, agreed to castrate Ouranos.

Gaia promised to make love with Ouranos but instead he was surprised by Cronus, who castrated him, with blood flowing everywhere. The spilled blood formed the avenging Erinyes, the Gigantes and the Meliae (ash tree nymphs). It is said the goddess Aphrodite was born from this seed spilling on the sea. From that day on the sky held its place and roamed no more.

CONNECTING WITH THE SKY ELEMENTS

Ouranos is a primal god of the sky, heavens and rain. The universe (space) is also his domain. Connecting with the sky means connecting with the air elements, which are great for communication and a feeling of inventiveness and expansion.

Take a blanket or pillow and go outside and *utiseta* (sit in nature) at any time of the day, as the sky is always beautiful whether dark or light. Lie back if you can and allow yourself a view of the sky. As you lie or sit, open up your senses one by one. Concentrate on one sense at a time and really try to experience that and that alone.

Look up at the sky; look at every detail. Take your time. Close your eyes and smell everything around you. What is on the air? Feel now. What can you touch, what are the hairs on your body sensing? Listen carefully; open your ears to the sounds around you. Take your time.

Ask for Ouranos to be present in his most loving form. Ask him to connect you to the most positive aspects of air, for example, the freedom, connection and effective communication, and that your voice will be heard. This whole process should be peaceful and connective. Take your time.

When you feel you have done as much as you would like, slowly disconnect from the openness of each sense one at a time. Give thanks to Ouranos and the elementals of the air. All things are possible now, so set some new intentions for yourself.

WHEEL OF THE YEAR:

Samhain

31 OCTOBER

There is much to love about Samhain (pronounced 'sow-en') or, as it's known more popularly, Halloween. It wasn't until I started down the witchcraft path that I realised Halloween wasn't a crazy American festival at all but an ancient Celtic one. Remember the Wheel of the Year is linked with seasons, cycles and their effect on the land, and our ancestors would be experiencing the first bite of winter. Everything would be dying back and fields would begin to lie fallow covered in snow and ice. Nothing grew. Death was visible and very near, with the elderly and sick suffering and perishing. It's no wonder Samhain became a festival of death, but of death as a part of the cycle of life. (If we observe where Samhain is on the wheel, Beltane – the festival of fertility and life – is its opposite.)

Samhain is a powerful time full of the magic of the restful void and of our ancestors; it is not a time of fear and barren emptiness. In fact, Halloween teaches us to laugh at death and not to fear it, bursting one of our last societal taboos. I always see Halloween as a chance to let everything I do not want to die back, so I imagine a fallow field in front of me resting, waiting and ready for whatever new possibilities I may wish to plant within it. Samhain is also considered the witches' new year because of this, so happy New Year!

Interestingly, pagans in the southern hemisphere celebrate Halloween on a different date than the usual 31 October because that date isn't the right time seasonally for those on the other side of the world; after all, we would be in spring and not travelling into winter. We flip the wheel and celebrate around the opposite date, 30 April, which is a far more suitable seasonal time for us as we are heading into the cold winter season. Besides going trick or treating, one of the most popular traditional activities to do at Samhain is to practise divination. We do this because there are two times of the year that the veils between this world and the spirit world are at their thinnest (the other night is Beltane). This means good-quality oracle work can be more easily done, with clear answers more readily available.

Getting in touch with our ancestors and friends who have passed is another part of Halloween, and although you would be tempted to think this could make for a sad evening it rarely does. We leave the most honoured place, the head of the table, for our 'dead guests', those who this night can join us in spirit and who will be remembered in joy. The honoured dead are served food and wine just as though they were there with us and are included in every aspect of the evening. They are remembered in laughter and gratitude.

4 Monday

Waning

5 Tuesday

Dark moon

It's a beautiful night for self-love. Stay in, treat yourself beautifully, journal, have a long hot bath.

6 Wednesday, ☽ new moon in Libra, 7.05 am EDST

Let's get honest: start afresh with intentions for extreme authenticity.

7 Thursday

Waxing

8 Friday ◗

Waxing

9 Saturday ◗

Waxing

10 Sunday ◗

Waxing

OCTOBER

M	T	W	T	F	S	S
			1	2	3	
4	5	6	7	8	9	10
11	12	13	14	15	16	17
18	19	20	21	22	23	24
25	26	27	28	29	30	31

11 Monday

Waxing

12 Tuesday

Waxing

13 Wednesday

Waxing

Wednesday is named after the Norse god Wodin (Odin).

14 Thursday

Waxing

15 Friday

Waxing

16 Saturday

Waxing

17 Sunday

Waxing

Lush you are, like a wild garden: untamed, fertile.

There is no fun trying to be anyone but yourself.

One only, like a precious jewel shining for all to see.

- THE GODDESS

OCTOBER

M	T	W	T	F	S	S
				1	2	3
4	5	6	7	8	9	10
11	12	13	14	15	16	17
18	19	20	21	22	23	24
25	26	27	28	29	30	31

18 Monday

Waxing

19 Tuesday

Waxing

20 Wednesday, ◯ full moon in Aries, 10.56 am EDST

A strong and powerful moon to sharpen your will, and the perfect night to set intentions for better communications with work colleagues, family and friends. Set plans in motion even if you are scared.

21 Thursday

Waning

22 Friday ◐

Waning

23 Saturday ◐

Waning

24 Sunday ◐

Waning

OCTOBER

M	T	W	T	F	S	S
				1	2	3
4	5	6	7	8	9	10
11	12	13	14	15	16	17
18	**19**	**20**	**21**	**22**	**23**	**24**
25	26	27	28	29	30	31

25 Monday

Waning

26 Tuesday

Waning

27 Wednesday

Waning

A good week to remove any unwanted hair, as it will grow back more slowly. This week discourages growth.

28 Thursday

Waning

29 Friday

Waning

30 Saturday

Waning

31 Sunday, Samhain

Waning

It's Samhain: happy witches' New Year!

A night of beautiful magic can be had. Yes, it's time to trick or treat and to scare away any fear of death! This is one of the two nights of the year where the veils between the worlds are at their thinnest, so it's a great night for divination of all kinds. Feast with your friends and don't forget those who have passed: set a place for them, pour them wine, leave them delicious food and speak about them.

OCTOBER

M	T	W	T	F	S	S
				1	2	3
4	5	6	7	8	9	10
11	12	13	14	15	16	17
18	19	20	21	22	23	24
25	**26**	**27**	**28**	**29**	**30**	**31**

NOVEMBER

- What would I like to create, experience and manifest this month?

_____

_____

_____

_____

- What are the important dates for me this month?

_____

_____

- What would give me joy this month?

_____

_____

- What am I devoted to?

_____

_____

- Ideas, musings, actions:

_____

_____

_____

SALACIA

GODDESS OF THE MONTH: NOVEMBER

The beautiful sea nymph Salacia was happy and content in her ocean home and kept a sea garden of beautiful corals and seahorses.

The king of all the seas, the great Neptune, saw her one day and set his heart upon her, wanting her for his wife. Salacia was chaste and virtuous and feared Neptune, for she had heard of his reputation. She was afraid he would take her away from all she loved or worse, so she hid from him in one of the furthest and darkest oceans.

Neptune had genuinely fallen for Salacia and meant no harm or disrespect to her. He searched for her but could not find her. He suspected she was afraid of him and sent his favourite dolphin to look for her and approach her. The friendly dolphin found Salacia and her seahorses, and Salacia explained her fears to the dolphin. The dolphin assured her they would be happy with Neptune and Salacia would certainly not lose the things she most loved; in fact, she may gain some new experiences and places.

The dolphin arranged a meeting between the couple, a meeting that would be fully chaperoned. After some respectful conversation and courting Salacia consented to marriage, and Neptune loved and honoured her as his wife.

Salacia was known by the finest pearls she wore in her hair, and she rode in a pearl shell chariot drawn by seahorses and dolphins to signify this most equal of unions. She kept all she had started with and Neptune granted her half of his kingdom.

Finding real love ritual

This spell is one of my most popular and one that has worked for many thousands of people, both male and female, of every sexual orientation. Don't skip on the preparation, though!

Have your intention clearly in mind or written down. I also advise you do some pre-thinking about your ideal partner, and create a list of the attributes that describe them. Include as much detail as you can think of and encompass the areas of personality, relationship type, connection, children, geography, interests, spirituality, physicality and values. For example:

I want a partner for a long-term relationship leading to marriage. He will be a confident man, open, loving and generous with his affection. He will be tall and take care of his body. He will be kind-hearted and happy. We will travel together.

I want a partner for a loving relationship. She will be vivacious and honest and have a laugh that makes me laugh. We will have long, lively, entertaining conversations about everything and nothing.

Nothing you write down will be wrong, but be very careful what you ask for.

Gather together a green or pearly white candle, a small shell or sea stone representing Salacia and paper and a pen. Cast and open a circle if you wish.

LIGHT THE CANDLE AND SAY OUT LOUD: *'I wish to attract my ideal partner quickly and easily.'*

TAKE SEVERAL DEEP BREATHS THEN SAY: *'Great goddesses and Salacia of the oceans, tonight is the beginning of something incredibly important. Tonight I will be attracting my ideal partner. This person is not my other half, nor will they complete me. They are an individual in their own right, yet they will come freely to me and will recognise that I am someone special and significant.'*

Read out your list, taking your time. Do this twice with lots of emotion.

Look at the candle or close your eyes and go within. Think about the person you have described, envisioning them in whatever way you wish. Hear their voice, feel their touch, inhale their scent. Imagine yourself doing things with them, from waking up to eating to sleeping to kissing. Do this in as much detail as your unconscious provides.

Be aware of how this makes you feel in your body: it should feel very good! Magnify this feeling: feel it warm you, pulse through you. There is so much anticipation in meeting this person now! The universe is still with you and is validating your choices.

HOLD YOUR SYMBOL OF SALACIA IN YOUR HAND AND AGAIN READ OUT YOUR IDEAL PARTNER'S ATTRIBUTES, PREFACING THE LIST BY SAYING: *'Salacia, hear my wish. This be the person that I desire; please take this intention and create with me so they flow toward me!'*

READ YOUR LIST OUT LOUD AND WITH FEELING ONE LAST TIME, THEN SAY: *'I know you will know me!'*

Thank Salacia and blow the candle out. Close your circle. Take the energised shell/sea stone and keep it with you as much as possible.

1 Monday

Waning

2 Tuesday

Waning

3 Wednesday ●

Dark moon

A powerful dark moon that can help take away old trauma. Transform!

4 Thursday, ☽ new moon in Scorpio, 5.14 pm EDST

Super new moon

There is no need to keep burning yourself out. Set intentions that will give you a combination of performance and peace.

5 Friday 🌓

Waxing

6 Saturday 🌓

Waxing

7 Sunday 🌓

Waxing

Like soft rain upon your skin, let love in.

- THE GODDESS

NOVEMBER

M	T	W	T	F	S	S
1	2	3	4	5	6	7
8	9	10	11	12	13	14
15	16	17	18	19	20	21
22	23	24	25	26	27	28
29	30					

8 Monday

Waxing

9 Tuesday

Waxing

10 Wednesday

Waxing

Harvest above-ground fruits and vegetables now.

11 Thursday

Waxing

12 Friday ◑

Waxing

13 Saturday ◑

Waxing

14 Sunday ◑

Waxing

NOVEMBER

M	T	W	T	F	S	S
1	2	3	4	5	6	7
8	9	10	11	12	13	14
15	16	17	18	19	20	21
22	23	24	25	26	27	28
29	30					

15 Monday

Waxing

16 Tuesday

Waxing

17 Wednesday

Waxing

18 Thursday

Waxing

19 Friday, ◯ full moon in Taurus, 3.57 am EST

Micro full moon

Partial lunar eclipse visable in New York.

You deserve beauty around you; find it. Set intentions to find comfort and beauty and an environment that supports you.

20 Saturday ◐

Waning

21 Sunday ◐

Waning

I love you more and more every day. Yes. Perhaps even every second.

– THE GODDESS

NOVEMBER

M	T	W	T	F	S	S
1	2	3	4	5	6	7
8	9	10	11	12	13	14
15	16	17	18	19	20	21
22	23	24	25	26	27	28
29	30					

22 Monday

Waning

23 Tuesday

Waning

24 Wednesday

Waning

25 Thursday

Waning

26 Friday

Waning

27 Saturday

Waning

Trim your hair now if you wish to encourage growth.

28 Sunday

Waning

NOVEMBER

M	T	W	T	F	S	S
1	2	3	4	5	6	7
8	9	10	11	12	13	14
15	16	17	18	19	20	21
22	23	24	25	26	27	28
29	30					

DECEMBER

- What would I like to create, experience and manifest this month?

_____

_____

_____

_____

- What are the important dates for me this month?

_____

_____

- What would give me joy this month?

_____

_____

- What am I devoted to?

_____

_____

- Ideas, musings, actions:

_____

_____

_____

NGI

GOD OF THE MONTH: DECEMBER

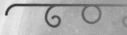

Ngi is a gorilla god and one of the four sons of Zamba, the creator god of the Yaoundé people of Cameroon in Africa.

All of nature, including the sky and stars, was made by Zamba except human beings. He decided to give that job of creation to his four sons, with the instruction they make man into their own image. His four sons were: N'Kokon, the mantis who was wise; Wo, the chimpanzee who was curious; Otukut, the lizard who played the fool; and Ngi, the gorilla who was strong.

One day Ngi was going about his business in the thick forest with his family of wives and children. A man decided he wanted to see Ngi for himself, as he thought he and his people may be stronger, so he followed Ngi to watch him. The man watched Ngi rule over his realm in nature with fairness and peace and share his food. He watched Ngi settle arguments and gently play with the young ones. The man didn't see Ngi display any great strength; all he saw were acts of peace and love. The man thought that perhaps Ngi was not strong at all and that perhaps he could take over his territory.

The man went into the clearing and threatened Ngi, who did not react to the man's threats other than to ask him go back to his own place if this was how he wished to act. The man continued to threaten the gorilla god. Finally, Ngi stood up to leave, and as he did so he picked up a huge stone boulder with one hand. He did not even face the man; he simply picked up the boulder, held it for a moment or two and then set it down. Then, without facing the man again, Ngi returned to the forest. The man realised that Ngi was indeed terrifically strong and that he has just witnessed true strength – the kind that has, at its heart, restraint.

Ngi demonstrates true peace and the idea that to seek or negotiate for peace is a position of strength, not weakness.

RITUAL FOR PEACE

We could all do with a bit more peace in our lives and within our communities. This spell can be done on any moon cycle and is particularly lovely to do outdoors, where you can put the water straight into the earth. Please ensure you will not be disturbed and that your phone is off. You will need a white or silver candle, a symbol of Ngi (a drawing or pic of a gorilla, a bunch of thick green leaves, a heavy stone) to place near you when you do the ritual and a large bowl of water.

Centre yourself, and breathe in and out deeply a few times. Relax; there is nowhere you need to be other than here right now.

Close your eyes for a moment and connect with the earth through your feet (or, if you are sitting down, through your bones). Feel your energy extend into the earth and then upwards and outwards through your body like a gentle hum of sound or electricity. When you are ready, open your eyes and light the candle.

SAY OUT LOUD: *'I call in peace today, son of Zamba, I call you, Ngi, to help me. You who embody peaceful strength, hail to you.'*

Imagine a lush, green forest with a crystal clear creek running through it (or another landscape that is peaceful to you). Imagine being within this landscape, opening all your senses. Perhaps animals are around you; perhaps Ngi is nearby. There is nothing at all to fear here, as everything is calm. Allow the energy of this peaceful place to enter you.

Take a big slow breath in, and breathe in the peace. Breathe out, extending the peace outwards towards the jungle, the sky and to all people, places and things.

SAY: *'I give peace to all. I give peace to myself.'*

THANK NGI FOR HIS ASSISTANCE, THEN OPEN YOUR EYES AND SAY: *'I offer the blessing of a peaceful flow.'*

Place your hands in the bowl of water and splash some upon the earth and flick some up to the sky, and place your wet hand upon your heart and then your forehead (mind). When you are done, spill the remaining water upon the ground.

WINTER

CUDDLE UP AND LET GO

If summer is our seasons of extroversion, winter can be viewed as being the opposite of summer, the season of extroversion. The shorter days and the cold weather make being inside more often more attractive. Throwing a log on the hearth, cooking beautiful hearty meals and cuddling up all cosy under the blankets – all these are deliciously wonderful winter-time activities that keep us contented by going inwards.

I like winter for its solitude. Where I live everything is much quieter and there are not so many distractions, and I am able to blissfully immerse myself in the planning of new things, writing, creating and dreaming of what is next as well as doing what is now. I get to take a breath and rest a while from the bombardment of life.

Some people dislike the extreme seasons of summer and winter because they can be, well, extreme! However, extremity is a good teacher: we learn resilience and how to balance ourselves in difficult situations. For those who live in places with a true icy and snowy winter, all this is magnified. Nothing grows under that snow; everything is resting, and the silence of snow will provide a huge respite to your senses. When you venture out the combination of the simplicity and beauty of the all-white landscape and doing something such as skiing or snow shoeing is fantastic. You get to open up your senses and engage with an extreme element, which is always life affirming!

For those who like working with deities, winter heralds the time when the underworld dark or ice gods and goddesses can be honoured. These are often deities who help us change what we don't like about our lives, who assist us to let go of old beliefs and grudges and who guide us gently forward through the darkness. You might enjoy working with Hekate, Hel, Persephone, Nuit, Osiris, Máni or the Morrigan. Those who love to work with snow or ice may appreciate Skadi, Ull, Freya, Khione, Boreus and Kuraokami.

TOASTING YOUR BURDENS

Next time you are sitting in front of a cosy open fire, why not try this: it's perfect to do solo or with friends.

Think ahead of time about what you want to get rid of and end up toasting (good examples are fears, burdens, misunderstandings and imbalances). Write these down on slips of paper.

Gather together a packet of marshmallows, sticks or wooden skewers and your slips of paper. Dim the lights and sit down, concentrating on the fire.

SAY: *'Universe, great element of fire, thank you for your presence. Allow me to toast a marshmallow or two. Enjoy!'* Focus on the fire: what does it look like or smell like? Feel the heat.

Pin a note on a skewer and hold it in your hand.

ALLOW YOUR FEELINGS OF THE BURDEN TRAVEL INTO THAT NOTE, THEN SAY OUT LOUD: *'I release this to the fire. IT IS TOAST!'* If you are doing this with others, they should cheer on the toasting to give you support. Repeat until all your notes are burned.

So it will be as you have asked!

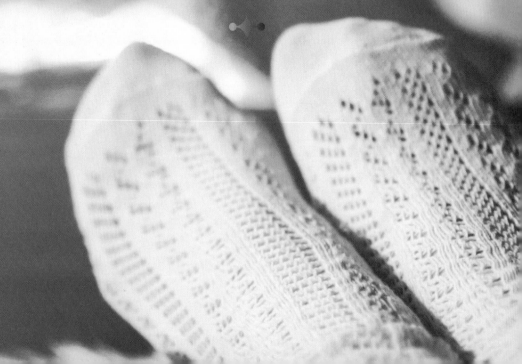

WHEEL OF THE YEAR

Yule, the winter solstice

21-23 December, 10.59 am EST

The Wheel of the Year has turned again and we find ourselves in one of the most joyous of festivals, Yule (or Yul in Scandinavian countries). Yule symbology is an easy one to link to Christmas with Christmas trees, snowy scenes, burning the Yule log in a big fireplace and the idea of a birth of light and hope over darkness.

Yule is a solstice festival, so it looks at where we are in the wheel within the cycle of light and dark. Yule celebrates the return of the light and warmth after the longest night. From this night on, after the winter solstice, the daylight hours will grow bit by bit. Light and warm – and life – will slowly return. This, the longest night, could be perceived as being a bright symbol of hope.

Gift giving is the gratitude of the season and the celebration of life. Magical talismans for good luck and prosperity are created on this night and given as presents to those we love. The famous Yule log is ritually burnt and the ashes are used later in other magical workings.

The ancient Norse peoples started the tradition of a special decorated tree that was bought inside. Rather than cutting down a tree, I decorate the trees in my garden with brightly coloured satin ribbons and solar-powered fairy lights and wrap up pretty crystals to entwine with the branches. Weeks before Yule many witches make handmade presents for their family and friends. Crafty people I know love to knit things and create beautiful paintings and cards, all bought into existence with intention and love; this is the heart of the festival.

Find a log-sized branch that a tree has discarded or buy some firewood. Consider what wishes you might have and prepare some little slips of paper. Ask everyone to write down their wishes on the paper, then pin them on or cut into the log so that the wood clips the slips like a wooden paperclip. Your log should be covered in amazing wishes!

Your special log is now ready to be transformed in the fire. Joyfully add it to the roaring fire in the fireplace, outdoor camp fire or fire pit. Everyone can sing or tell each other of their wishes or hopes; all should be supportive of each other. There is often cheering as the Yule log goes whooshing up in flames, such is the happy energy of knowing your wishes are coming to you!

29 Monday   November

Waning

30 Tuesday

Waning

1 Wednesday   December

Waning

2 Thursday

Waning

3 Friday ●

Dark moon

The last dark moon of 2021: let it all go, clean it all out!

4 Saturday, new moon in Sagittarius, 2.43 am EST

Super new moon

Blossom! Open yourself to the new: ideas, beliefs, different ways of getting something done.

5 Sunday ◑

Waxing

Another year we are together. Go round the sun, riding the moon and loving all in between.

– THE GODDESS

NOVEMBER						
M	T	W	T	F	S	S
1	2	3	4	5	6	7
8	9	10	11	12	13	14
15	16	17	18	19	20	21
22	23	24	25	26	27	28
29	30					

DECEMBER						
M	T	W	T	F	S	S
		1	2	3	4	5
6	7	8	9	10	11	12
13	14	15	16	17	18	19
20	21	22	23	24	25	26
27	28	29	30	31		

6 Monday

Waxing

7 Tuesday

Waxing

8 Wednesday

Waxing

9 Thursday

Waxing

10 Friday

Waxing

11 Saturday

Waxing

12 Sunday

Waxing

You are part of the all, swirling and dancing, kissing eternity with every breath.

– THE GODDESS

DECEMBER

M	T	W	T	F	S	S
			1	2	3	4	5
6	7	8	9	10	11	12
13	14	15	16	17	18	19
20	21	22	23	24	25	26
27	28	29	30	31		

13 Monday

Waxing

14 Tuesday

Waxing

15 Wednesday

Waxing

16 Thursday

Waxing

You might like to prepare your wishes and celebrations for Yule, coming next week!

17 Friday

Waxing

18 Saturday, ○ full moon in Gemini, 11.35 pm EST

Micro full moon

The last full moon of 2021: make it count. Set intentions for your personal growth and the reduction of fear in your life.

19 Sunday

Waning

DECEMBER

M	T	W	T	F	S	S
		1	2	3	4	5
6	7	8	9	10	11	12
13	14	15	16	17	18	19
20	21	22	23	24	25	26
27	28	29	30	31		

20 Monday ◐

Waning

21 Tuesday, ◐ Yule, the winter solstice, 10.59 am EST

Waning

Happy Yule! This solstice reflects the shortest day of the year and the longest night. Hope breaks through the darkness. It is a traditional feasting time and one of the best times to make charms and talismans for abundance. Make delicious mulled wine and burn a Yule log with your wishes attached.

22 Wednesday ◐

Waning

23 Thursday ◐

Waning

24 Friday ☽

Waning

Christmas Eve

25 Saturday ☽

Waning

Christmas Day

26 Sunday ☽

Waning

There is wisdom in sometimes being still. Doing nothing is doing everything.

– THE GODDESS

27 Monday 🌘

Waning

A good few days to remove any unwanted hair, as it will grow back more slowly.

28 Tuesday 🌘

Waning

29 Wednesday 🌘

Waning

30 Thursday 🌘

Waning

31 Friday

Waning

Last night of the year: catch the positive wave of power of the new year (check my Facebook page for the free annual Ride the Wave Ritual Event). Let go of what was and ready yourself for new momentum. Ensure you have your intentions set for 2022. Mark the end of this year with a ritual of gratitude before you head out to celebrate. At midnight, connect with that wave of new hope and know that your resolutions will come to fruition. Mark the moment with a kiss, a dance or a sip of champagne. Spill a little on the ground for Jana, the goddess of the new year.

1 January 2022 Saturday

Waning

Welcome to 2022!

2 January 2022 Sunday

Waning

Delight in yourself.

– THE GODDESS

DECEMBER							JANUARY 2022						
M	T	W	T	F	S	S	M	T	W	T	F	S	S
		1	2	3	4	5						1	2
6	7	8	9	10	11	12	3	4	5	6	7	8	9
13	14	15	16	17	18	19	10	11	12	13	14	15	16
20	21	22	23	24	25	26	17	18	19	20	21	22	23
27	28	29	30	31			24	25	26	27	28	29	30
							31						

NOTES AND MUSINGS

REORDER FOR 2022 LUNAR DIARY

Name...

Address..

City.......................................State.................

Postcode...................Country.......................

Phone...

Email..

Mastercard ☐   Visa ☐

Credit card number...

Name on card...

Expiry date: ....CVV number...............

Please send me .... copies of

2022 Lunar Diary

USD$19.95 / GBP £17.99 per copy

To place an order in the USA
Red Wheel/Weiser/Conari
65 Parker Street, Suite 7
Newburyport, MA 01950, USA
Toll Free: 800.423.7087
orders@rwwbooks.com

To place an order in the UK
Simon and Schuster UK
1st Floor
222 Gray's Inn Road
London WC1X8HB
United Kingdom
Tel: +44(0)20 7316 1900
Fax: +44(0)20 7316 0332
enquiries@simonandschuster.co.uk

2021 MOON PHASES:
UNIVERSAL TIME CHART

If you don't live in Australia and don't wish to convert times from Australian timings, here is a handy chart that gives moon phases in universal time (UT). It is the mean solar time for the meridian at Greenwich, England, used as a basis for calculating time throughout most of the world.

DARK MOON	NEW MOON	FULL MOON
12 January	13 January, 5.00 pm	28 January, 7.16 am
10 February	11 February, 7.03 pm	27 February, 8.17 am
12 March	13 March, 10.21 am	28 March, 5.48 pm
11 April	12 April, 2.30 am	27 April, 3.31 am
10 May	11 May, 6.59 pm	26 May, 11.13 am
9 June	10 June, 10.52 am	24 June, 6.39 pm
9 July	10 July, 1.16 am	24 July, 2.36 am
7 August	8 August, 11.50 pm	22 August, 12.01 pm
6 September	7 September, 12.51 am	21 September, 11.54 pm
5 October	6 October, 11.05 pm	20 October, 2.56 pm
3 November	4 November, 9.14 pm	19 November, 8.57 am
3 December	4 December, 7.43 am	19 December, 4.35 am

RESOURCES

Here is a list of handy moon-, earth- and pagan-related resources that I particularly like:

www.paganawareness.net.au: if you want more information on paganism or witchcraft, this is a great place to start. The Pagan Awareness Network Inc. is a not-for-profit educational association with members Australia-wide that is directed by a management committee whose members are drawn from a broad cross section of the pagan community. It has no formal ties with any religious body, but works pro-actively both within the pagan community and as a point of contact for the public, including government and media organisations. PAN aims to continue as the Australian pagan community's most effective networking and educational body.

www.themodernwitch.com: this is my website and contains loads of free resources and downloads, witches' tools and a store from which you can obtain books, downloads, blessed talismans and temple beads, including lunar beads. Register for the free newsletter.

www.natureluster.com: this is my site about the benefits and wonders of an earth-centred life. Try the Natureluster program.

If you are interested check out the many fan pages that have been set up for gods and goddesses that you can join.

LUNAR WEBSITES

eclipse.gsfc.nasa.gov/phase/phasecat.html: NASA site that provides historical and current information about moon phases. It is wonderful for researching your lunar return.

www.timeanddate.com: great for lunar timing/equinox information.

www.smh.com.au or *www.theage.com.au:* some of the best tidal information comes from popular newspapers such as the *Sydney Morning Herald* or *The Age*.

www.green-change.com or *www.moongardeningcalendar.com* for moon gardening.

CONNECT ON SOCIAL MEDIA

f   staceydemarco, Stacey Demarco's Lunar & Seasonal Diary Page

⊙   @themodernwitch

ABOUT THE AUTHOR

Stacey Demarco, the Modern Witch, is passionate about bringing practical magic to everyone and inspiring people to have a deeper connection with nature. Stacey has been teaching for more than 20 years and is the author of the best sellers *Witch in the Boardroom*, *Witch in the Bedroom*, *The Coffee Oracle*, and *Plants of Power*, all of which have been translated into multiple languages. She is also the co-writer of *The No Excuses Guide to Soul Mates* and *The No Excuses Guide to Uncovering Your Purpose*. Her oracle cards decks include the best-selling *Queen of the Moon Oracle*, *Divine Animals Oracle* and *The Elemental Oracle*, both illustrated by Kinga Britshigi.

Stacey is the founder of Natureluster, which educates and works to reconnect people to the health-giving power of nature. She is also an animal activist, ethical beekeeper and dedicated adventure traveller and lives by the beach in Sydney with her husband and furry companions.

Stacey provides private consults, teaches workshops and leads the popular Wild Souls naturelusting retreats nationally and internationally.

Learn more at *www.themodernwitch.com.*